Smart Marketing for Solopreneurs and Microbusinesses

By
Douglas Freeman
Ideascape, Inc.

Copyright ©2018
Douglas Freeman
Ideascape, Inc.
All rights reserved.

Printed in the U.S.A.

No part of this book may be reproduced or transmitted in any form or by any means, electronic or mechanical, including photocopying, recording or by any information storage and retrieval system, without written permission from the author.

ISBN 10: 1725083213
ISBN-13: 978-1725083219

Cover photo by Edward van Buuringen.

DISCLAIMER

The author has made every effort to ensure that the accuracy of information in this book was correct at time of publication. He does not assume and hereby disclaims any liability to any party for any loss, damage or disruption caused by errors or omissions, whether such errors or omissions result from accident, negligence or any other cause. Nothing written or implied in this book should be taken or construed in any way as legal or regulatory advice. The methods described in this book are the author's personal thoughts and those of his contributors. They are not intended to be a definitive set of instructions or professional advice. Readers should seek legal advice or other professional assistance with regard to business formation, licensing, regulations, accounting and legal document development.

DEDICATION

I dedicate this book to the millions of solo and microbusiness entrepreneurs across the globe. They sustain economies, drive innovation, and provide extraordinary services to their clients and customers. Plus, they enjoy the personal satisfaction of building valuable enterprises that they can call their own.

TABLE OF CONTENTS

INTRODUCTION 1

QUESTIONS TO SET THE STAGE FOR MARKETING 3
1. What Business Are You In? 5
2. Do You Have a Workable Business Plan? 7
3. Have You Established a Brand? 9
4. What's Your Professional Value? 11
5. Do You Use Industry Knowledge as Marketing Knowledge? .. 13
6. How Adaptable Is Your Business? 17
7. Are You Continually Learning? 19
8. Do You Sabotage Your Marketing? 21
9. Do You Know That Failures Don't Define You? 23

TOOLS TO SUPPORT YOUR SMART MARKETING 25
10. Construct a Marketing Action Plan 27
11. Create a Marketing Resume 31
12. Develop a Capabilities Statement 33
13. Build a Professional and Business Platform 35
14. Customize Proposals for Your Services 39
15. Include Marketing in Contracts and Agreements 45

ESTABLISH YOUR MARKETING POSITION 47
16. Market Your Value Proposition 49
17. Sell Your Soft Skills Along With Your Expertise 51
18. The Best Pathway to Clients 53

19. Competitive and Realistic Rates 55
20. Discounting Rates for Marketing Purposes 59
21. Marketing Angles to Reduce Income Volatility 63
22. Marketing Remote Services 67
23. On-Call Services as a Package 71

SMART MARKETING TIPS 75
24. Market to the Right Prospects 77
25. Target the Right Types of Projects 79
26. Niche Services to Penetrate Markets 83
27. Scaling Your Business for Opportunities 87
28. Referrals and Inside Tracks 91
29. Prospect Research to Increase Pitch and Proposal Success 93
30. Pitching Your Services at Interviews 97
31. Customer Service as a Marketing Tactic 101
32. Conversations With a Touch of Marketing 103
33. Leveraging Client Interactions to Expand Services 107
34. Hidden and Subtle Marketing Opportunities 109
35. Proposing New Project Ideas to Clients 113
36. Packaging Your Services 115
37. Options to Work With Cash-Strapped Clients 117
38. Pitching Solutions to Prospects 121
39. Strategic Use of Content Marketing 125
40. Online Contract Applications 129
41. Marketing Your Services Through Agencies 131
42. Online Freelancing Platforms 133
43. Marketing to Government Agencies 137
44. Co-Working Space Use for Client Prospecting 141
45. Opportunities With Project Wrap-Ups and Post-Mortems 143

CONCLUSION 147
46. Your Marketing Success Formula 149
47. About the Author 151

INTRODUCTION

What is smart marketing for solopreneurs and microbusinesses? Smart marketing is providing your unique combination of skills, experience and knowledge to clients based on customized approaches—a form of relationship marketing. Smart marketing includes using adaptability, resourcefulness, customization and value-based promotion as a competitive advantage. This is how you, as a solopreneur or microbusiness, can build mutually beneficial, lasting relationships with clients you serve.

In over 30 years of business as a solo communication services professional working with organizations ranging from startups to Fortune 100 corporations, my mission has been to provide extraordinary value to my clients. The result? I've worked with the majority of my clients for years, not just days or weeks on single projects. I've been paid fees commensurate with the quality of work I've delivered but also for the additional value I've provided them.

Additional benefits my clients receive include alerts about opportunities that I become aware of, introductions to contacts I think it would be advantageous for them to know, industry news related to projects and observations/insights I pick up on as I learn about their organizations. This is what collaboration and mutually beneficial relationships are built on. I'm rewarded for this by loyalty, a continuous flow of new projects and sometimes by extra payment for this value-added time. My value-added services are kept at a reasonable level and strategically applied to ensure that my time and expertise are respected by my clients.

The marketplace for professional services by solo and microbusinesses is changing rapidly. A growing number of services are being commoditized. That is, services such as certain types of public relations, advertising, accounting, marketing, project management, human relations and any number of other business functions have been transformed into whatever-as-a-service. Typically, the lowest cost and minimum-acceptable-quality provider wins the job. It's unlikely that you can compete with this model and maintain a profitable, sustainable business.

Your competitive advantage is to offer the strategically designed, value-added, customized services that set you apart from global lowest-cost competitors. You can focus on being the high-value competitively priced vendor who is more like a partner to your clients than a faceless one-off service churning through an endless series of single projects to eke out a living.

As a result, you must understand that there are marketing implications and aspects in nearly everything you do as a business. This ranges from the name you operate under to the proposals you submit to clients you target to how you wrap up projects. In other words, your marketing strategy can be to embrace every possible opportunity to build long-term relationships with clients. This also includes creating an ecosystem in which you are a visible and desirable solution provider within your market niches.

You can market your business this way, no matter what field you're in or industries you serve. In this book, I'll share my best tips on a wide range of marketing activities you can engage in today to promote and sell your value to the clients you'd prefer to work with.

QUESTIONS TO SET THE STAGE FOR SMART MARKETING

1
What Business Are You In?

To name the business you're in seems so obvious, especially with your experience and skill sets. You're in the business of graphic design, insurance, financial management, motivational speaking, management consulting, executive coaching, product design or whatever. These are standard job descriptions for what you do in your business, right? Well, maybe.

An associate of mine had been in the public relations (PR) business for many years, but wanted to move on to something new and more personally meaningful than PR. There was the challenge. I asked him to describe the business he has been in. "Communications, publicity planning and strategizing, event management, promotion of clients to target media," he said. Certainly, those are functions in PR. But do they actually describe the business he has been in?

I asked him to consider looking at his work more globally. What's at the foundation? What about considering it from the perspective of the outcomes of that work? In general, he's a client visibility optimizer. At the foundation, he's a connector and relationship builder. The outcomes include revenue enhancement, opportunity cultivation and credibility elevation.

The upshot was that his business could be defined more broadly than by his PR experience alone. If he were to start his own business, it could be associated with PR but not be PR. For example, he's very talented at connecting people for mutually beneficial relationships. He could provide consulting services on successful connection-making techniques, create mixers or meet-ups to coordinate brain trusts, match professionals or businesses with complementary needs, speak to groups on creating business relationships, or blog on relationship building for a target audience such as startups. Yes, there really are companies and professionals who do this. It's often categorized as a form of marketing consulting even though there's far more to it than what would be defined as marketing.

As you launch or build your business venture, take some time to consider the business you're in from as many perspectives as you can. Disassemble the functions or elements of the general job description you're using. Go beyond those pieces to recognize particular talents you have that are associated with the activities common to your type of work.

There likely are more ways to use and present your skills and knowledge than you realize. And that new way of thinking might shape your business in a way that differentiates it from others and positions you to focus on the functions you enjoy the most. This will help you market more effectively to the right audiences.

Knowing what business you're in also should be integrated with your branding efforts. Use that information to communicate your exceptional and unique value to target audiences. Chances are this will set the stage for you to communicate your level of experience, knowledge and skills in a better way than before.

2
Do You Have A Workable Business Plan?

I'm always amazed at how many solopreneurs and microbusinesses don't have even basic workable business plans. These are plans that address their branding, business focus and services, marketing, and business case for existing (i.e., is there a market for their services?).

They have many excuses. The most common one is that they aren't sure what goes into a business plan and would rather focus on "doing" instead of planning. Rarely do they want to spend precious funds to pay for assistance in developing a plan. There's also an impression that a business plan must be an elaborate presentation, as you'd need to prepare for an investor.

Guess what? You are the investor in your business—with time, money and resources. If you'd want to examine a business plan for a new venture before investing money in it, why wouldn't you want the same for your own business?

I propose a compromise by using the lean startup methodology. A key approach within its framework is to create minimum viable products (MVPs). An MVP often is a bare-bones first version of a product to test with prospective customers. If it solves a problem effectively—there's a need for it—you devise a more complete version to build a business with it. If it doesn't resonate with prospective customers, you've failed fast. This prevents risking everything and investing a huge amount of time on one idea that has little chance of success. The same process applies to services, not just physical products.

This is an effective approach to develop a business plan for a business like yours, considering the fact that you are the product for your venture. A minimum viable business plan addresses the key aspects regarding conceptualizing and operating your business. To draft a minimum viable business plan is not an overwhelming or highly complex project to undertake.

An important thing to remember is that you aren't committing to a permanent plan that dictates all you do in your business. It's a flexible, adaptable presentation of your business and what you'll do. Consider it a living document that will change as you make your way forward. This plan doesn't need to be perfect nor all-inclusive. *Minimum viable* are the operative words here.

In one or two pages, your plan should simply and clearly explain your branding, business niche, services, pricing, initial marketing activities and the opportunity or need for your services. This is so you know where you're heading with your business and how to get there. Many entrepreneurship experts also suggest that you include your desired monthly or annual income goal so that you have a target to work toward.

A big advantage of writing down the elements of your business plan is that it makes you think through your business concept and what you anticipate doing to make it work. It may be a pain to write a business plan, but it'll prevent issues down the road. With each element of it, keep asking yourself, "Why does this make good business sense?"

3
Have You Established a Brand?

What's your brand? Marketing experts describe a brand as the image and substance you present via your Web site, printed materials, services and products, and communications. In many ways, it's how you operate and why you do it a certain way. Your prospective clients perceive your brand as your mission or personal cause for being in business, the value you offer, your quality and credibility, as well as what differentiates you from your competition.

It's easy to think of a brand being specifically about the type of business you're in and the marketing of a particular service or set of services. In some industries, brands are represented by nothing more than job titles. Branding messages usually revolve around the application of skills and knowledge of professionals to solve customers' problems. Unfortunately, this doesn't do enough to differentiate businesses from their competition.

We could say that everyone from construction managers and trainers to writers and video producers all do the same work as others in their field. The challenge with branding services like these is to establish ways to stand out and apart from everyone else. This helps you become visible to target prospects, establish yourself as the professional to whom others refer their contacts and the business your desired prospects seek as the go-to person/people with solutions to their unique needs.

Because of the value you have to offer your clients, you are the brand. Ideally, your story is one of integrity, positive results, deep knowledge, expert guidance, personal attention, passion, effectiveness, trustworthiness, resourcefulness and empathy. You are the professional whom clients want to hire and work with because of who you are, why you are in business, how you operate and the value you provide. Your brand is built on your story, which is core to the solutions you provide.

The name of your company or its pitch (perhaps its slogan) reflects how you are different than others in your field. Your mission statement presents your unique approach to your business and what you strive to accomplish for clients. In all of your messaging, you communicate your value within the context of your relationships with clients. One way to address this is to answer the following question: What makes your business especially meaningful to prospective clients?

Understand that branding isn't stuff that you just make up. Branding that works is all about authenticity. Customers can tell if a brand is created just to sell or one that's manufactured purely as a marketing device. Your customers are investing in you and the value of your services, so they must see evidence of your brand in everything you say and do. Inconsistency is a credibility killer.

Here's an effective way to help you define or confirm your brand. If you've worked in an industry for a fair amount of time, it's likely that you've established a personal brand with colleagues and clients. Try asking some of these people how they would describe your business or professional brand. You might even incorporate parts of their statements in your branding image and messages.

When developing your branding image and messages, just be sure to think beyond sales. Focus on the human side of what you do and what you're known for in your industry. Build a brand that attracts the types of clients you want to work with, the projects you desire and, importantly, the long-term relationships necessary for a sustainable solo business.

4
What's Your Professional Value?

Discussions with my associates who also run solo and microbusiness often get into questions about our professional relevance. We ask, "Are we positioned to be in-demand and marketable in our industry niche?"

In the spirit of building a business case regarding your relevance, here are some specific benefits that likely apply to professionals like you in a wide range of services and industries:

- Skills as a leader of people and organizations.
- Experience developing products and services, along with lessons learned in the process.
- Proficiency in marketing products and services, internally to stakeholders and/or externally to customers.
- Sensitivity and skills in being an advocate for customers.
- Experience with project management.
- Life experience in coping with adversity and success.
- Perspective about business trends, management philosophies and cultures.
- Experience with business, product and service life cycles.
- Skills related to forming and sustaining partnerships and alliances.
- Appreciation for responsive and value-based customer relations.
- Capability to analyze and identify valid evidence to evaluate products and services.
- Experience pitching startups or legacy businesses to strategic partners and investors.
- Understanding about business growth issues and solutions.

- Access to extensive networks of relevant contacts.
- Patience and perspective responding to change within organizations and in industries.
- Professional resourcefulness from business experience.
- Credibility within the industry or a related one.
- Cultural sensitivity from experience and values.
- Appreciation of loyalty and commitment.
- Understanding of the power of actions, not just talk.
- Knowledge about the value of planning and knowing that all plans are dynamic.
- Experience with failure and turning lessons learned into positive actions.
- Skills collaborating with diverse teams.
- Capability to mentor or coach clients with regard to institutional and industry knowledge and business skills.

This list should serve as a reminder to you about points you can make if you're in a situation that requires you to present your relevance to prospective clients. However, the real value of these points lies in you connecting them to your business profile. In other words, match your skills, knowledge and experience with each point to re-frame your business relevance.

Career coaches and advisors often have their clients perform self-analysis exercises like this. The objective is to help their clients shape their business ventures and develop messages to convey during pitches and in proposals. It's also a way to remind their clients of what they have to offer in the marketplace. Too often, we don't appreciate these value points unless we make an effort to explore them directly.

5
Do You Use Industry Knowledge as Marketing Knowledge?

You don't know what you don't know. And what you don't know can mean marketing opportunities are lost. How effectively you keep up with your industry and developments outside it can affect how you market your services and to whom you market those services.

I keep up with news and trends within my profession and industry in several ways. It's amazing how informative posts are from industry colleagues on social networks. Also, I'm fortunate to have a large network of contacts who regularly share valuable information, insights, observations and news. Valuable information comes to my attention through my membership in special interest groups on social networks, representing a broad number of fields. This includes articles, posts and content shared from members' sources.

For general profession related news, I subscribe to quite a number of daily, weekly and monthly news and information reports. Sources are industry or sector related publications, companies, business organizations, specialized journalists, educational institutions, and subject matter experts.

What should you look for? This depends on the news and content you need to keep up as an informed professional and to customize your marketing efforts for your niche. One objective should be to follow news and content that support your skills and knowledge. This is content that makes you feel like you know what's going on in your business ecosystem, but also motivates you and inspires ideas. Another objective is to keep up on trends related to projects you tend to seek and the types of clients you want to pursue. What do you need to learn to anticipate clients' needs? What should you know to be able to have meaningful conversations with colleagues and clients about their projects?

The other key area to keep up on is your prospective clients. Define your needs by asking a broad range of marketing questions. Where is your future work going to be coming from? What developments will best help you adapt to changing market conditions and the directions your clients' industries are headed? What are emerging pain points for your prospective and current clients? What opportunities are arising from prospective clients just outside the traditional edges of businesses in your industry?

If you want to serve a specific group of companies or organizations, you should keep up on them. Use news search utilities or RSS feeds for online publications to provide you with alerts when articles or news releases are published. I automatically receive summary reports that contain headlines and links to sources on companies according to key words or phrases that are relevant to my marketing efforts. Look for online services or individual publishers that provide these feeds. Also, you can "follow" companies on many social networks to receive their news, articles and posts.

When I run across news or information that is actionable, I usually do a bit more research to figure out what steps I can take to adjust my marketing efforts. In some cases, I'll note contacts to follow up with to see if they can use my services. I use other alerts as prompts to devise strategies to reach out to or connect with new markets or prospects. Some news or information helps me know what to follow for future investigations and marketing actions.

I check my email, news and social networks daily for valuable information. Over the years, I've cut down the number of summaries and alerts I receive due to quality, relevance and timeliness of the content. However, I also add new sources as they come to my attention. It's critical to stay on top of this effort because you don't want these messages to pile up and become an overwhelming task to address. Don't set yourself up for information overload. Be selective.

Try starting with only a handful of feeds that include the most valuable sources clearly related to your profession and industry. Include a few general sources that offer a bigger picture of interesting news and trends, as well. Be careful not to be hyper-focused on your field or you might be blindsided by impacts from developments on the periphery or outside your field or industry niche.

Only you can determine what's necessary to know to keep your business thriving and marketing messages on target. Your goal is to position yourself on the leading edge in your field by keeping up as a professional as well as staying aware of broader market opportunities.

6
How Adaptable Is Your Business?

Changes in the scope of job functions, where work is conducted, how work is performed and the ways that workers are managed are being re-imagined daily. The nature of work itself is changing and that means your marketing must be adaptable.

So how do you plan for the unplannable so your business survives and thrives? Maybe you don't. Perhaps you're better off asking a different question: How do I shape my career, business and marketing at this point to adapt to constantly changing work and economic conditions?

I've always been inspired by associates who have sustained adaptable, entrepreneurial careers for decades. Their interests and curiosity, new opportunities, changes in the marketplace, and client requests guide their business transitions. In my case, these same influences change what I do through my company, resulting in co-founding startups and even providing chances to acquire equity in another entrepreneur's ventures.

The way I've done this and adjusted my marketing efforts concurrently has been by pursuing continuing education, doing a lot of reading, listening more than talking, experimenting in new fields, being alert to opportunities, as well as accepting some risk and failure. I firmly believe that we must adopt entrepreneurial thinking and adaptable businesses to succeed. Your marketing flows with this mindset.

There are many marketing benefits from positioning yourself for an adaptable career to spot opportunities and operate at the forefront of trends. How many of the following actions are you taking regularly?

- Reading about trends and developments within and on the fringes of your current industry and areas of expertise.
- Listening to colleagues, influencers, friends, network contacts, clients and leaders inside, as well as on the periphery, of your profession and industry to pick up on emerging needs.
- Consistently adding new skills and knowledge to enhance your ability to successfully pursue opportunities.
- Interacting with and expanding your business network to position yourself for referrals, references, offers and advice.
- Experimenting with your career by testing new interests in different ways within and outside your areas of expertise.
- Building your personal brand and marketing yourself or your business to prepare for lost clients, evaporating contracts and shifting marketplaces.
- Developing a flexible mindset with your career so that you always are devising ways to make it align with future changes.
- Asking probing questions about your own and industry assumptions, the relevance of your expertise, the future of your clients, etc. to prevent a wondering, "Why didn't I see that coming?" in the future.

All of these actions can help ensure that your marketing efforts are adapting to fit the evolution and expansion of your services. There's great value in adopting a startup style entrepreneurial mindset. This is because you are the product and service competing for relevance and value in the changing marketplace.

Adaptability will help you thrive in the chaotic intersection of business and marketing.

7
Are You Continually Learning?

Like any professional, you must work to stay relevant to your clients and market. This means you must stay current with the skills necessary for the market's needs and knowledge about developments and trends in your industry. If you don't keep up, you risk obsolescence. And your marketing must reflect all of this in obvious and subtle ways.

An example of keeping up regards using collaboration platforms. There are many of these platforms used to manage aspects of projects ranging from calendars and shared documents to conference calls and customer relationship management. If you aren't familiar with the ones your market uses, you'll be presenting a barrier to getting hired. These are the tools your prospective clients may use—ones they expect you to be comfortable using.

Your skills likely need to be enhanced on an ongoing basis, especially in industries where certifications or special tools are required to perform work. The nice thing is that you can find training for almost anything online. If not, be sure to keep up on trends and take any available courses. A good source for direction and offerings in this area is your local or national professional organization(s). I've had outstanding learning experiences through meetings, presentations, workshops and conferences via several organizations.

You might find great value in attending industry and related industry conferences. This can be an efficient way to stay current on skills, knowledge and trends. It also affords you opportunities to network with colleagues and prospects. In some cases, you might invest your time and money to build connections and familiarity with certain events to set yourself up as a future speaker or panelist.

Attending conferences can be costly, so I suggest that you choose them strategically. I consider conferences that provide solid training through workshops on trending skills or topics, networking opportunities with target clients, the chance to meet prominent experts in my field, and ideally visit a location where I can conduct other business activities.

Sometimes you can recognize trends in your field and industry by reading, through conversations with people in and outside your field, and by listening to clients. It's easier to just keep up than to position yourself a step ahead, which is more valuable. Therefore, you must ask the right questions to a diverse group of individuals at the right times.

An effective way I've found to become aware of trends within my industry and those that potentially could affect my industry is through startups. I follow startup developments via various online news and notification services. I'm constantly asking: What's going on here? How could the activities of these startups affect aspects of my industry? And, how these startups affect my target clients? Then, I ask how I can move in those directions with my services and marketing.

Additionally, I engage with startup founders and teams through networking and outreach efforts as potential clients. When I provide services to startups, I also ask plenty of questions and make observations to learn from those interactions for marketing purposes.

Within your marketing communications, you want to indicate how you're staying ahead of the curve in your field. Specifically, this can be touched on in your Web content, proposals and conversations with prospective clients.

8
Do You Sabotage Your Marketing?

We've all had good experiences and bad ones. We've developed our own biases and stubborn positions. Also, there are the limitations in skills or knowledge depending upon changes in our industry. All of this results in personal or professional baggage that can be revealed accidentally in our marketing efforts.

Do you tend to overly rely on marketing messages that tout what you've done too far in the past and how you've done it? Do you have excuses for not keeping up on skills, knowledge, technology, industry trends, etc.? Do you have attitudes—preconceived notions and experience-rooted biases—about colleagues and clients? Do you avoid types of projects or clients due to bad experiences with them in the past? Do you have a chip on your shoulder for whatever reason?

I warn my associates to dump the baggage or it'll be very challenging to succeed in business. That's because hints are exposed in marketing content and in conversations. There's nothing wrong about pursuing the types of clients, projects, working relationships and other preferences that fit your mission and business plan. It's just important to watch out for exposing your negative attitudes and projecting the image of closed thinking to prospects.

How can you minimize the most harmful baggage? Consider some training to improve your weaker skills. Study trends in your field and industry to focus your services and tune into your market niche(s). Keep up on trends regarding communication, collaboration, project management and industry-specific tools. That way, you don't feel it necessary to mask worries about your value in the marketplace with counterproductive attitudes or limitations on how you conduct or market your business.

Think of it this way, you're aiming to be hired because of the expertise you have to offer. That marketing approach represents good outcomes for customers. You must present yourself as a positive thinking professional who gets things done successfully. There's no room for introducing negative messages or impressions in this proposition.

There are plenty of challenges we face when building and maintaining our businesses. It's disadvantageous to add your own self-destructive baggage to the mix. Project the attitudes that you would look for if you were in your clients' shoes. Focus your marketing messages on the "world" you strive to create for your clients.

9
Do You Know That Failures Don't Define You?

I'd venture to say that every entrepreneur has experienced failure. It's part of the landscape even for the most successful businesspeople.

This isn't to say that our entire business ventures fail all the time. Far more often, particular marketing efforts or types of services just don't take off. Sometimes the market changes and we cannot compete any more. Clients pivot in ways that exclude us from their needs. There certainly are occasions when projects fail, through missteps by us or circumstances beyond our control.

If you've conducted adequate market research that has verified needs for your solutions for a category of client prospects and you are qualified to serve them, you should be able to successfully market your business. This means you're able to package, price, present and provide your services in ways that meet clients' needs. Adjustments and adaptations always will be required to remain competitive. Yet, a total misread of the market or a big shift within it that no one could see coming might blow your entire business model out of the water. Such events certainly can lead to complete misses on marketing messaging.

A failure must be taken as a temporary setback. The lessons learned will be used with the next incarnation of that business or marketing effort. There could be instances when what seems like an unrecoverable failure actually is a sign that a solo business isn't a great fit for you. That's when your pivot may be to find the right partnership to establish, even if the business is different than what you tried alone.

Very often, the difference between those who ultimately succeed and those who give up is resiliency. It's the ability to learn from failures and setbacks. They use that knowledge to set out in a different direction or use the experience in a positive way. Failures are information, feedback. They aren't personal or professional indictments.

In fact, there may be ways to tell the story about a failure as part of a marketing case. How did you turn around what wasn't working with an effort or project into a winning reboot? This reflects how you respond to a negative situation through skilled analysis, resourcefulness and a commitment to success.

Self-employment is a journey of course adjustments while conducting your business. As a nimble solopreneur or microbusiness owner, you're positioned to experiment continuously and aggressively. Succeed or fail fast. Failing fast means that you don't sink your business by sticking with an unsuccessful effort too long. There should be a point where you can step back, evaluate what you're doing and decide if it makes business sense to proceed longer, make adjustments or ditch the effort.

There's no magical formula for determining which action to take. I suggest that you examine milestones and make a thoughtful business case for which path to choose. Failing or encountering setbacks isn't fun. It's easy to become frustrated and wonder if you'll find the right formula to build a sustainable business and marketing platform in the years ahead.

However, with resiliency you can navigate your way through setbacks to end up accomplishing great things. Be pragmatic. Prepare, strategize, act, succeed or fail, learn, move forward with improvements, and repeat. This is the path to coping with failures as best you can, so you can focus on building the business you envision. Imagine the benefits of incorporating this attitude in your marketing messages.

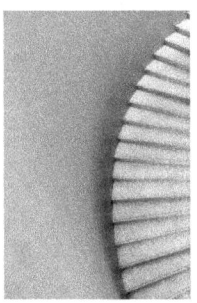

TOOLS TO SUPPORT YOUR SMART MARKETING

10
Construct a Marketing Action Plan

A minimum viable business plan should address your marketing strategy in at least a bare bones manner. However, you need a more detailed marketing action plan to ensure that you're efficient as you continually promote your business. This includes marketing experiments as well as updates to your strategy.

Developing and using a marketing action plan helps you maintain a focus on priority activities and stay organized to be able to measure results. It takes a more strategic approach these days to navigate the barriers you face when marketing your services, including the rapidly changing marketplace. My point is that a thoughtfully constructed marketing action plan can increase the efficiency of your marketing activities.

What does a typical marketing action plan contain? Think of this as a priority list in two sections. One section is a list of perhaps five to 10 major marketing efforts that span six months to a year, listed from highest priority to lowest. Just because an effort is ranked lower doesn't mean it's not important to address. The only marketing efforts on this list are ones that must be acted upon during this time frame. For example, efforts might include using content marketing on specific social networks. The objective is to reach out to certain target prospects to elevate your visibility, increase incoming inquiries and open communication channels that might expose business opportunities.

For each of your major marketing efforts, you should complete the second section with daily or weekly actions to support those efforts.

These are your to-dos or checklists to ensure continuity of your marketing, during slack times and even busy times.

For example, actions listed under content marketing could include posting one original article and two brief posts per week. These should be developed from a content production idea list that you maintain. It should expand as your reading and work spark ideas that you note for reference. Perhaps you aim to research and pursue one speaking engagement each week from your frequently updated list of future conferences and industry or professional organization events. To-do items might include emails or calls to organizers as well as submission of proposals.

Also, you might chip away daily at target company contact lists to get referrals for projects, submit introductory pitches to prospective clients using target lists or complete proposals for prospects you've had communication with previously. It's likely that a fair portion of your daily or weekly marketing time will be spent researching prospective clients and networking with contacts so opportunities to take specific marketing actions are revealed.

How you track your marketing actions to keep up on the status of each depends on what works best for you. Many of my associates use customer relationship management (CRM) software or their own databases to accomplish this. I've tried several of these tools and each has its advantages and limitations. What works best for me these days is a simple word processing table because I have very focused marketing efforts. This is linked to a contact database to record all contact/company names, position titles, email addresses, phone numbers, Web sites, social network URLs, etc.

Typical information to record in your database includes the following: contact identification and communication information, how and why you connected with the person, dates for all interactions, notes about interactions including marketing action details, reminder dates for follow-ups, and ideas for further networking or marketing that may or may not relate specifically to this person. I also add the names of my contacts to whom I could introduce these people as a professional courtesy.

The goal of a marketing action plan is to ensure that you work efficiently, continuously and purposefully over time. That said, this plan must be adaptable as changes are called for due to trends in results and especially from unanticipated opportunities. I've had to drop everything at times, including marketing actions. Typically, this was to take on an emergency project, compose a proposal for a time-sensitive opportunity or communicate with prospects from referrals because of limited opportunity windows. As soon as possible, I catch up on missed action plan items though.

11
Create a Marketing Resume

What's the difference between an independent business professional's marketing resume and a job hunter's resume? Both appear to market an individual's skills, knowledge and experience for certain types of work within the scope of a defined role.

The differences may seem subtle, but these really are two very different marketing pieces. Unfortunately, most people are accustomed to developing job resumes rather than business marketing resumes. As an independent business professional, you are pitching your credentials for a single project or series of projects typically over a set period. You aren't presenting an argument for what a valuable long-term employee you would be, how you'd work for a company exclusively, grow with their enterprise and potentially move up within their ranks. As an independent professional, you're pitching a business entity that serves many clients in multiple ways with the background intention of working with them over a long period.

Compensation, work processes, responsibilities and other relationship characteristics are quite different for outside professionals. In other words, your business model is completely different than that of someone looking for a job. Marketing resumes essentially present a business case for someone with your professional assets to provide solutions tailored to specific prospects.

In my experience contracting with companies and government agencies, most don't ask for resumes as a starting point for consideration. They've been referred to me, checked my Web site, reviewed my social media profiles or previously had some type of communication with me. Therefore, most have expected my credentials or qualifications to be included as a section in my proposals. They don't necessarily care about my complete work history. What they want is my work history that's relevant to the specific project they have. This would be my track record working on similar projects and maybe with similar types of organizations. Just as no two proposals I draft are the same, the resume sections are never the same.

I've been successful using marketing resumes that include descriptions of projects presented like very brief case studies. These included the name of the client (if permitted), work or problem I addressed, how I provided solutions, which skills were used, and the final outcomes of my work. All of this is highly customized for relevance to the prospective client, the nature of the project and my skill set. The level of detail depends on whether the work discussed in these cases was covered by non-disclosure agreements (NDAs). If so, the information can be generalized so as not to improperly reveal details.

It seems that nearly all online contract job platforms require submission of a resume for profiles. Some can automatically pull information from your social network platform profiles. This process can be unreliable due to the type of information your profile contains and how you structure the presentation of it. Part of the reason for job platforms' reliance on resumes is that they're stuck in the employment (job) model instead of a business-to-business marketing model.

Good marketing resumes also include information that shows how we keep our skills up to date and add new ones, expand our knowledge, work with diverse clients and companies, and use the communication and technology tools our clients use. This is proof that we're relevant and valuable as contract professionals.

12
Develop a Capabilities Statement

The business version of resumes are capabilities statements. I've found these to be quite useful in my marketing efforts, especially when seeking contracts with government agencies and large corporations.

Typically, a capabilities statement is a one-page presentation. It concisely covers the following:

- Your business emphasis (main category and services).
- Core competencies.
- Very briefly described—and relevant—projects.
- List of current/recent clients.
- Relevant business achievements and awards.
- Professional association memberships.
- Licenses and accreditations.
- Business classification categories (e.g., NAICS codes).

For federal government prospects, you might want to indicate your registration with the System for Award Management (SAM) and North American Industry Classification System (NAICS) categories.

Think of your capabilities statement as a neatly organized business brochure without any fluff content or graphics.

I've used general purpose versions of capabilities statements focused on a specific type of service or group of services most often. There have been occasions when I tailored this document for particular prospects and types of contracts to emphasize certain credentials or experience. I customized the brief company profile, types of services and list of clients to be especially relevant for a particular agency and type of project.

Capabilities statements are great to attach to initial inquiry responses as well as with proposal submissions. You might even consider including a downloadable version on your company Web site as a marketing tool, if appropriate for your services and prospects.

13
Build a Professional and Business Platform

Visibility tends to produce opportunities. A drawback of working only in a narrow niche in your particular field is that it likely insulates you from opportunities outside your normal business circles. This results in your lack of visibility beyond the types of work and audiences of prospects within those circles.

There are simple methods to increase your visibility to attract new business or connect with new audiences who can move you in the directions you want to go. One of the most important ways to accomplish this is to develop a business platform. The components of platforms vary by industry, the type of work you do and the audiences you wish to reach.

For example, let's say you're a video producer-director who mainly works with advertising agencies on commercials. You'd like to position yourself for opportunities to work on a greater variety of projects, such as live events, documentaries, crowdfunding videos, low-budget films, media for e-learning programs and long-form marketing videos. You have the transferable skills and knowledge to successfully handle these projects—maybe even have dabbled in them over your career. Unfortunately, you're known in the advertising community but invisible to these other production and client communities. How do you build a platform that will increase your visibility to such target audiences?

I know producers-directors who use a variety of activities to develop their platforms. They re-design their Web sites to creatively pitch how their experience in one area of production has prepared them well for the other types of productions they want to tackle. Some have even produced and directed personal projects or took on pro bono work to be able to show examples.

Another platform related strategy for them has been to speak at events to groups who include prospective clients in those new project areas. Writing articles and social network posts on subjects related to new types of projects can help create an interested audience and reach target prospects. Some producers-directors have even launched creative multi-media marketing campaigns to get on the radar of new target audiences. These included podcasts, series of videos posted on multiple platforms and social networks, crowdfunding efforts for their own or others' projects, online magazines, creative email campaigns, engaging mailers, blogs, and business-social events for face-to-face contact.

Before you launch efforts to create your platform, conduct a little research. Clearly identify the individuals you want to reach, by their job titles, work focus, compatibility in style and clientele, typical budgets, subject matter or products they deal with, and any other factors that ensure you're concentrating on the right audience(s). Next, figure out how to reach them through your platform as part of your marketing plan. Business-to-business and business-to-consumer outreach are different. Figure out how to get in front of prospective clients' eyes, be listened to, meet in person or be referred to by their trusted associates. Tailor your efforts and methods to sub-groups within your target audiences, if that boosts your visibility.

An additional way to build your platform is to serve as a connector for new and existing contacts. By making introductions, you build relationships but also subtly market yourself by increasing your visibility. This is one of the greatest values of your network. Don't ignore the many ways to benefit from it.

Your visibility platform is not a one-off effort. It's an ongoing campaign tied to your branding. Think of professional speakers who write articles and books, serve as news experts, appear on TV shows, produce podcasts, create training videos, etc. They're always looking for ways to reach target audiences and build their number of followers.

Look at what others in your field do to support their platforms. Try the same strategies and add your unique twists to differentiate your business from the competition.

14
Customize Proposals for Your Services

I think it's fair to say that developing proposals is one of the most dreaded tasks for independent professionals. Although professionals likely have written or processed many proposals over their careers, that experience likely doesn't make writing them any easier. Although the intent of proposals is sales, they also serve as marketing pieces.

First, it's critical to understand that presenting a proposal for contract work is quite different than applying for employment. Prospective clients are looking for specific solutions from professionals whom they believe can deliver results and fit their budgets. For contractors, it's our skills, knowledge, experience, solutions and project-specific value that count, not our "permanent" value as an employee.

Secondly, you must commit to the time investment to prepare effective proposals. It's tempting to minimize that investment of time by taking shortcuts such as using generic or boilerplate proposals with little customization. I've developed many successful proposals for my services as well as for clients. Also, I've seen many proposals prepared by small businesses and large companies. The vast majority of these proposals were very general with what looked like a few "blanks" filled in to adapt them to the prospect. This is an incredible waste of time and resources, too often based on quantity rather than quality.

As solopreneurs and microbusinesses, we just cannot afford to play a numbers game with proposals. We'll end up spending all of our time writing them and not getting paid for the services we want to deliver.

I want to stress two main messages here. First as I mentioned previously, focus on quality over quantity. Only propose your services to clients you want to work with as well as for the projects you want and ones you're at least reasonably qualified to handle. This approach alone increases your odds of being awarded contracts.

Second, make your investment of time count. You must conduct some research about prospects to understand who they are, what they do, how they do what they do, their mission, their market position, information related to their pain points and even their history addressing needs related to your type of services. This is the only way you can speak intelligently about their needs for their project and impress them.

You cannot just try to get proposals out the door to prospects and worry about the specifics of their needs in the interviews. The fact is that you won't get to the interview stage by submitting incomplete and unprofessional proposals—ones that don't sell them on your services. Personalize and customize proposals. Even offer preliminary ideas for solutions to their pain points. Like in sports, preparation is what produces victories.

Generally, there are two types of proposals: unsolicited offers for your services and submissions in response to requests for proposals (RFPs). Both must be customized via proper research. For unsolicited proposals, you want to generally sell your services but customize elements for each prospect. Therefore, you should address the prospect's range of pain points that your services (solutions) address and all of your relevant qualifications to show that you're a perfect fit for them.

For RFP submissions, your focus shifts to customizing your content for the specific projects and contexts for your work with that organization. Never submit incomplete RFP documents. Answer every question, fill in every blank entry space and provide every piece of information they request. There's no thinking, "I'll give that to them later" or room for accidentally not including elements. Incomplete proposals usually are deemed non-responsive and not considered for the contracts.

Considerable effort is required to become skilled at developing proposals, even with years of business experience to rely on. It's important, though, because proposals and pitches will play a major role in determining your success.

This brings us to another component of proposals. According to job hunting experts, the value of cover letters is up for debate. Yet, for independent professionals pitching their services via proposals, cover letters can be powerful sales and longer-term marketing tools. They give you a chance to quickly convey messages that might not be covered in your resume or CV, capabilities statement or application form. I encourage you to use cover letters to accomplish the following:

- Emphasize how your knowledge, skills and experience are especially appropriate with the project and client.
- Mention information that reflects how much you know about the company and understand their needs.
- Touch on the personal and professional reasons why you want to work with the client and on the project.

Communicate your "why me/us proposition" in the introduction section of proposals. All proposal writers should find a way to state their mission or cause. This is why you are in business on a personal level. The reason is there is an emotional element in the hiring of contractors. If your cause aligns with that of the prospect, it frames your services as a good fit with the client's business vision for their current project but also beyond that. Over the years, I've learned that a deciding factor on being awarded many contracts was that the client and I had similar missions. I had to be fully qualified for the work, of course, but that X-factor was an important connection.

A specific question that is often ignored is how much to give away in proposals about the solutions you have to offer. Yet, a way to elevate the persuasiveness of a proposal is to provide a taste of your initial ideas regarding how you might address a prospect's needs. Such hints show that you've invested significant thought to the prospect's needs. It's a way to clearly connect the value of your services to the prospect's pain points. I've found that these ideas can be great conversation starters in follow-up communications and interviews—the longer-term marketing efforts. This requires some time, but it can separate your proposal from those of your competition.

One of the most annoying challenges is silence from prospects after submitting a proposal. Your first thought might be that your proposal was rejected and that the prospect is unprofessional and inconsiderate not to respond with that news. Although that might be the case occasionally, you actually don't know what's going on behind the scenes with a proposal recipient or the company. You don't know what you don't know.

I've experienced delayed responses to my proposals due to prospects' sudden personnel issues, budget changes, company mergers and acquisitions, changes in needs, and other factors. Occasionally I followed up with my contact by email or phone to check on the status of my proposal and learned the reason for the delay on a decision. Other times, I just moved on with other work until I heard back. I've rarely experienced permanent silence.

In several cases, I was contacted months after my submission. The prospect finally was ready to move forward on the contract. An important lesson here is not to jump to conclusions when you don't hear back about proposal submissions. I strongly suggest that you never publicly or privately criticize companies if this occurs.

You also must appreciate the importance of learning from successes and failures. It's frustrating to make the effort to prepare great proposals and not know why we didn't win. Many contracting managers are hesitant to explain their reasons to you due to the risk of disclosing something that could expose them to complaints or lawsuits. For this reason, I try to learn as much as possible about why I had successes. My clients have been very open about specific factors for their decisions. That information can help you refine your proposal development.

Finally, you want to be sensitive to the marketing value of proposals. Whether or not you get the project, your proposals communicate many things to decisionmakers. A well-prepared proposal reflects your professionalism and the competitive position of your business. It may present your value for a specific type of project, but it also includes other information about your services and approach to working with clients. All of this adds up to marketing messaging. You might be approached directly for future projects, be referred to others in the company or even be recommended by proposal reviewers to businesses that company works with.

If you're concerned that your proposal writing is not in top form, seek assistance from an experienced proposal writer or take a course on proposal writing. Also, there are many books on proposal development for various business sectors and industries.

15
Include Marketing in Contracts and Agreements

Taking the time to establish contracts and agreements with clients is a necessary business step for every solopreneur or microbusiness. It's a subtle part of your marketing because it supports the perception by clients that you conduct your business in a competent and transparent manner. You can promote the way you onboard clients with contract establishment to reflect credibility and professionalism.

One of the core purposes of these documents is to detail exactly what services are being contracted. However, this doesn't mean that you cannot include a small section that lists the additional services you provide that are related to the project—an upselling opportunity now or in the future. You can clearly point out that these services are not included in the scope of work but may be included after authorization by the client.

As a marketing element, include brief descriptions of the optional services maybe even with estimated costs. For example, a consultant might list a few project implementation tasks tied to what would normally be guidance alone. Just state that any or all of these services may be included in the contract's scope of work via amendments.

Because you already have the contract at this point, it's important not to use sales type in your language. Your goal is to offer extra options as a courtesy. Ideally, the list will motivate your client to ask you questions about the services and potentially expand your work on the project.

There are many great resources from attorneys and business advisors that spell out the elements of proper contracts and letters of agreement.

I'm not qualified to offer legal advice on this subject, so my thoughts on this subject cannot be taken as such. Also, certain professions and industries may require very different types of legal documents due to intellectual property protection, liability issues and other factors.

My contracts and agreements are fairly standard for the communications services and consulting industry. Five of the most important parts of these documents are: a clear description of the project, scope of work, schedule, costs and payment terms.

The description of the project ensures that my client and I agree on the nature of the project, general process to take place and the final deliverable(s). A detailed scope of work makes it clear what the client is paying me to do. This helps prevent scope creep or misunderstandings about milestones or the work process. A mutually agreed upon schedule manages expectations on steps and timing of deliverables.

For my client's budgeting perspective and my business requirements, all hourly, flat fee, expense and other costs are listed. I never want a client to assume anything about the cost of doing business with me. Payment terms clarify how, when and how much I'm paid.

The "additional options" section is placed near the end of the document, as it's somewhat like a supplement. I've seen that a few of my associates in industries such as media production, project management and graphic design include options in the statement of work section. I prefer this content to be presented at the end so it doesn't appear to be an obvious effort to upsell my clients.

Contracts and agreements are critical for small businesses. If there are changes to the project, client management, circumstances related to the project or unexpected events during work, your contract or agreement will protect everyone's interests. Good contracts or agreements are a hallmark of professionalism.

ESTABLISH YOUR MARKETING POSITION

16
Market Your Value Proposition

It's easy to question the value of your skills, knowledge and experience. I've been there. It was when work became scarce, I lost a major client or I felt burned out of providing certain services. This is one of the dangerous situations that can paralyze you, so you stop doing the marketing work that you must do to stay afloat.

Self-doubts can creep in quickly. You might start imagining all types of negative scenarios of what could happen. That's when it's time to step back from the emotional minefield. Instead, think about why you decided to become an entrepreneur and your credentials to support your decision. Your focus must shift to an all-out marketing mode.

First off, your value as perceived by prospective clients often depends on the quality of the solution(s) you're offering and how you communicate that in your marketing. The more impact your solutions can have with a client, the more your work will be valued. Can you save them significant time, money, resources or prevent problems? Will you help them make more money, attract better employees, engage more customers, work more efficiently and effectively, increase the value of their business, improve their products, help them create something new, etc.?

Those questions present the value proposition of your marketing communications. To consider this another way, look at your business from the perspective of your past satisfied clients and those who respect your work. That way, you know how valuable you'll continue be to your present and future clients.

Another marketing mindset regarding your value has to do with who you are as a professional. Don't underestimate the skill set you have to offer. Your previous job titles likely don't reflect all of the services you actually provided.

For example, a sales representative does far more for a company than just seek out and secure transactions. The job includes functions such as customer feedback curator, the company's face in the industry (e.g., industry relations and marketing), product development consultant, industry networker, trend analyzer, business communications specialist, project manager, sales event producer, conference speaker, opportunity spotter and personnel recruiter. These are all marketable services, individually and as a service package. Again, this is more evidence that you offer great value.

If you need an exercise to better recognize your professional value, make a list of every function you've had in your career. After completing your list, cluster the skills you want to emphasize in the marketing of your primary business services. Match those services to the "pain points" of your prospective customers, as you'd define them in your business plan. The fact that you offer those solutions to known needs of prospective clients means that you clearly offer value in your marketing messages.

All of this should help reassure you that you have professional value that others will pay for. It's why they'll trust you to solve their problems. And it's why you can feel confident that you've launched a viable business that can be marketed to target audiences.

17
Sell Your Soft Skills Along With Your Expertise

Clients want effective solutions from a professional like you. They need your knowledge, skills and experience—your job-specific hard skills—to address their pain points. However, in the past several years I've learned that my clients have begun to appreciate qualities beyond the hard skills normally associated solely with being qualified for types of work. Those "other" qualities are called soft skills.

Soft skills often are described as qualities associated with interpersonal skills and professionalism. These include communication skills, listening skills, empathy, creative thinking, problem-solving, critical thinking, time management, decision-making, flexibility and adaptability, as well as motivation and teamwork skills.

It can be challenging for service providers to reveal soft skills in capabilities statements, resumes and proposals. To just say that you have a checklist of soft skills somehow doesn't come across as verifiable because they're not measurable or concrete like hard skills. It's easiest to show your strengths and authenticity related to soft skills during personal interactions, such as interviews, live pitches, conversations and project discussions.

One of the best ways to do this is through stories. By this, I mean stories of projects you've worked on, organizations you've worked with, professional growth you've experienced or industry issues to which you've given considerable thought. How did you manage challenges? What interesting experiences did you have working with clients or colleagues? How have you coped with successes and failures? Why have you written about certain subjects? Notice how questions like these expose to who you are as a person and as a professional. They also are indicators of how you communicate and collaborate with others.

Stories that touch on these characteristics may be included in cover letters, introductions in proposals, case studies of projects you've worked on, your Web site content, content marketing and anywhere else you present your services. Be careful not to make this content personally or emotionally over-the-top, like the over-sharing we see too often on social networks. It's business information on a humanistic level. After all, a big part of hiring decisions is emotional, often considered a part of "fit" in an organization.

The trick that I've used to provide prospective clients with an impression of my soft skills is to arrange preliminary conversations. We discuss the project and the services I can provide. But, I always try to frame appropriate messages within the context of soft skills.

For example, I'll bring up my experience with a project similar to the one the prospect needs addressed. My snapshot description won't just present the facts such as I did this to solve that and these were the measures of success. I'll touch on the process that took place, with its challenges, interactions with others and how issues were resolved. Within this context I'm able to express soft skill qualities. Another way to touch on soft skill characteristics is to relay thoughts about the similarity of your business missions, customer service commitment or connections to your communities. This is what you could do in your introductory emails or messages.

I'd suggest that you devise creative ways to integrate your soft skills in your marketing efforts. I believe you'll have a competitive advantage over those who don't understand the importance of these skills and how they affect hiring decisions.

18
The Best Pathway to Clients

All independent professionals have choices about the types of work, groups of clients to serve and industries to focus on with their business. At some point, they must decide to focus their marketing on following either the path of least resistance or pursuing a planned direction.

The path of least resistance refers to continuing the same type of work with the same group of clients in the same industry as you've been involved with in the past. A related but slightly different case is when you tend to accept opportunities that arise by default. Many times, it's easy to go with the flow and not fight battles to seek something different.

For example, let's say you've been a project manager in commercial construction for many years. You could let your business replicate that same work, relying on your existing contacts, companies and types of projects. Opportunities likely would surface after you let everyone know that you're now available independently. If this is the business you want, that's great.

A planned direction is focused on intent and specific marketing actions. This is the type of work, group of clients and industry you really want to focus on that in some way relates what you've done in the past. In most cases, you can't rely on opportunities just popping up spontaneously.

Using the project manager example again, let's say you want to move into project management for environmental restoration. Now, you must establish your visibility with a different set of contacts and organizations in this different industry. Your existing contacts certainly can be of assistance if their projects cross into your target market. They can provide referrals to people they know who could use your services. However, this new direction demands far more effort to pursue. If it's the direction you want to go, it's worth the extra work to seek it.

This isn't an either/or proposition. You can balance these two approaches if you're careful not to diverge from the direction you want to go. I must admit that I've fallen into the trap of veering to the path of least resistance several times. I was offered lucrative contracts doing work I previously said I wouldn't do again. Sometimes, this decision was due to laziness. Other times, I rationalized it because I was helping out a former client or associate with whom I had a good relationship.

While these choices were good for business income, they did distract me from efforts to secure the types of work I very much wanted to pursue. I might have missed great opportunities in my target field while I worked on these easy-to-get projects. I felt a bit of guilt because I wasn't doing what I knew I should be doing and eased up on my marketing to my preferred types of prospects.

If you're in the early stages of building your business, you might have to accept the path of least resistance to survive. There's nothing wrong with that. But, if the point of creating your business was to work in a different field or industry, be sure to not abandon that effort. Stick to the core intent behind your business plan.

Ideally, be all-in whether the path of least resistance is your choice, you plan on building a very different business or if a blend of these two approaches makes good business sense. This will bring clarity to your marketing efforts.

19
Competitive and Realistic Rates

One of the toughest business tasks for any type of professional is to establish rates to charge clients. Your level of skills and knowledge—proven expertise—represents significant value to the clients you serve. Although you likely don't specifically market yourself based on your rates, they do play a part in the types of clients you wish to seek and your marketing approach.

In some fields, such as consulting, the link between value and cost often isn't a major barrier. Performance and outcomes are what drive contracting decisions by clients. Sometimes this is a function of supply and demand. It also can result from needs that require highly-specialized expertise or unique situations such as emergencies.

Value and cost usually are considerations for the majority of professions and across most industries. A variety of factors must be taken into account to set hourly or project rates. These include your overhead costs, minimum acceptable rate, professional credentials, how specialized your services are, location and competitors' rates in your target client market. All of this adds up to your value proposition, which is reflected in the range of our rates.

Overhead costs are too often ignored when setting rates with too big a focus on the marketability of your services. Costs of doing business must be included in rates for a sustainable business model. Ongoing expenses may include phone, Internet, equipment, business service subscriptions, professional services, electricity and gas, auto expenses, rent (even for home offices), supplies, advertising, insurance, etc. This is a baseline amount before adding the cost of your services.

Your minimum acceptable rate is the rock bottom hourly or project rate you'll accept unless there's a very compelling marketing reason to work at cost or a loss. Any fee below your overhead costs is working at a loss even if you're willing to charge nothing for your time.

Professional credentials range from the years of experience in your field and level of expertise to degrees or certifications and client history. Let's say that your credentials elevate you to the top 10 percent of people in your field. Your rates should be in the highest range compared to competitors. This is a key component of your value to clients and must figure into your value proposition that's communicated in your marketing.

If you have highly specialized skills, knowledge or experience, that justifies higher rates. A top expert in a specialty field likely is paid considerably more than a generalist in that same field. Again, it's about the value you bring to your work and, therefore, to your clients.

It's unfair, but true, that your location can be a limiting or advantageous factor in setting your rates. For example, professional services rates on the two coasts of the U.S. traditionally have been higher than in the Midwest or South. However, the cost of living can be higher in these regions. Working remotely and living in a low-cost area of the country can be a competitive advantage with lower costs. Yet, it might be more challenging to charge higher-end rates commensurate with your level of expertise. It's a good idea to consider your clients' locations when you formulate your rates, to be competitive while balancing overhead costs and appropriate rates.

As a professional, I urge you to compete on the value you have to offer rather than just on rates. Competing mainly on rates, therefore being paid less and working many more hours a week, is a sure way to run yourself out of business. You cannot compete against free or minimum wage workers, wherever they're located. It's just not a viable marketing tactic due to the long-term financial consequences.

Check the rates of comparably qualified contractors in your area and nationally who serve your groups of target prospects. Calculate an acceptable range that's the basis for a profitable business model. Then, make your value proposition the core of your marketing efforts. When price becomes an issue, first offer streamlined or fewer services. Focus on what you can do for prospects based on their budgets, avoiding the temptation of discounting your services when negotiating contracts.

20
Discounting Rates for Marketing Purposes

It seems that everyone expects a deal. Depending upon the nature of your work and industry you serve, there's a good chance that you'll be asked to discount your rates. Also, you may be tempted to work for low rates to build your clientele or generate some cash flow. This can be a big issue in your business if you want to establish the policy of payment commensurate with your business credentials.

An associate of mine described a scenario that came from her experience soon after launching her business. As she pitched a growing number of prospects for her services, many of them said they were interested but her fees were far higher than what they saw on online job platforms. They said that those other consultants were willing to take on initial projects at very cheap rates. Her prospects didn't consider lowest cost providers much of a risk due to their cheap rates.

My associate said that she was tempted to match those deals or offer a discount to at least compete with them. After she thought about her extensive experience and high-value services, her decision was to not play the discount game. She could offer verified expertise, a far more engaged relationship, high confidence that her work will exceed clients' expectations and competitive rates for professionals with her experience. Her concern was that by greatly discounting her rates she could risk setting a precedent that would put pressure on her to lower her rates again for these and future clients. Her experience was core to her value proposition. High value costs more than low value.

The three most common scenarios for discounting our fees for marketing purposes are: (1) Promises of future work if your rates are cut on the first project, (2) pitches about "great exposure" in exchange for discounted rates and (3) requests for pro bono (donated) services.

Although promises for future work if an initial project rate is discounted may be well intentioned, this is a bad bet the vast majority of the time. I've fallen for this several times on projects I was particularly interested in working on or with clients I thought had a lot of potential for long-term relationships. The future work never, I repeat never, came about. Most often, this is a ruse to pay as little as possible to get high-value work.

The other risk with this is that they may very well request continuation of your discounts on future projects since you already set the precedent of cheapening your services to accommodate their "needs." If they can afford your full rates later, they can afford them at the start. I suggest that you'd be better off pitching fewer or simplified services to clients instead of initial project discounts.

Promises of great exposure if you discount rates for work is code for "we don't want to pay you" or "we have no money." Your work has value for clients. Working for free is not a sustainable business or marketing model.

That said, there are cases when investing your services with a client might make sense. For example, a client might commit contractually to promote your name or company to their audience. If their audience size or target audience fits your marketing plan, then a test may be worth it. Discounting or trading services can work in cases when it's very likely to be mutually beneficial.

Startups tend to be the most frequent adopters of the exposure for work approach. In those cases, consider asking for equity in exchange for a defined period of free or discounted services. Another option is to establish an agreement for deferred payment, with a set number of months in the future when they have revenue. My best advice is to only enter into these arrangements strategically, not just on hopes and promises, and negotiate the best deal you can. You can shape your marketing to such prospects so these options are presented up-front.

Pro bono work makes sense when you want to support a non-profit with your time and expertise rather than a monetary donation. I've found occasional pro bono work very rewarding as a way to give back to my community. There's often some type of recognition for this which can increase your visibility and be used for marketing purposes but that really isn't the point. Be aware that once the word gets out that you offer your services like this to organizations, you may be contacted with requests quite often. Pro bono work becomes part of your marketing identity, locally or nationally. Except in rare circumstances, I limit myself to one or two pro bono projects per year.

In conclusion, offering discounts is a legitimate marketing tool when used strategically. Just understand that discounts can erode your perceived value in the marketplace, not just secure contracts. Used too often, a lower profit margin could very well affect the sustainability of your business.

21
Marketing Angles to Reduce Income Volatility

Being an independent professional means that you accept the risk of income volatility no matter how effectively you market your services. You have good months and tough ones; sometimes good years and those not so good ones. Diversification with multiple income streams can be the key to enhance revenue stability for your business.

The main reasons to establish multiple income streams are to stabilize your revenue and even generate passive income. There are great benefits of pursuing one or both of these efforts to prevent income gaps and ever-changing markets. This is a very important part of your overall marketing strategy.

Diversifying your income generating activities involves developing multiple income sources in connection with your core work activities paid to you as hourly or project fees. Passive income is revenue that's not as dependent on or completely independent of the hours you work. Think consulting hours versus online fees for access to a training program you developed based on your field of work. This passive income fulfills the common definition of entrepreneurship, which involves building a business bigger than yourself or your hours worked.

How do you accomplish this? Any or all of the following marketing-centric activities can diversify your businesses:

- Adding services – If you're a specialized professional, you may wish to diversify your services. Do this by looking for elements of your work that can be transferable to other categories of services or to different target clients. Continuing education may be a route to offering new skills. Listen to clients and study your industry to identify pain points that you could address and develop new services as solutions. I started my business offering only one service, but over time that grew to well over a dozen different services. This has been the case for most of my associates, as clients asked for help in new areas, opportunities arose to apply skills for different projects and the types of projects that interested them changed.

- Consulting – If you provide services, look for ways to repurpose your knowledge and skills in the form of consulting. I was drawn into consulting by clients who used my project related services but then wanted me to advise them on areas of planning, strategy development and project management. I have numerous associates who found that guiding others to perform work activities better was more challenging and rewarding than offering those services directly—helping them do the work rather than doing the work for them.

- Training – Consider developing live training services, built on your experience and knowledge, such as workshops or courses. If you create an online training program, it can generate passive income from enrollments due to auto-delivery of the program. I've offered a variety of live training services leveraging specific skills I have. Some of my associates teach part-time at local colleges as well as offer workshops through professional organizations and at conferences. Also, some solopreneurs have such success with their training packages or presentations that they "franchised" them by licensing others to deliver that training. This is a way to build a business far larger than your solo enterprise.

- Writing – Find opportunities for paid writing related to your expertise, such as articles, columns, guest blogging and co-authoring. If you write a book about your work experience, you can generate passive income from sales. For several years, I was a business journalist writing for many publications as I provided technical writing services to clients. I and quite a few of my associates have written books for the income and because books are great marketing tools.

- Speaking – If you're comfortable speaking to groups, you can earn significant income from keynotes at clients' internal meetings and at industry conferences. Recordings of speeches and presentations can generate passive income online through downloads or training packages. Speaking has raised the visibility of many of my associates in addition to revenue. Their visibility increased offers for contracts for their services and positioned them for opportunities to move their businesses in new directions. Paid speaking is a way to significantly increase your earnings per hour. That can mean that you have the choice to reduce your hours spent on your typical client services.

- Video blogs and podcasts – Your knowledge and industry perspective have value. Video blogs and podcasts are popular ways to monetize this value through subscriptions. Having a large network of contacts is a big advantage, as you can start with or market to a significant audience. Quite a few of my associates have had such great success with podcasts that they've chosen to cut back on their other work. Plus, the exposure from broadcasting content resulted in many other business opportunities. Monetized video blogs and podcasts are great examples of building passive income.

- Products – Depending upon the work you do and industry, you might have insights into physical products you could develop and sell. I've known management consultants who have created business games and creative tools that teach collaboration and other skills. A real estate expert I know teamed with software developers to create applications for professionals in his industry. Sales of products create passive income and help build a business that's not dependent on selling your hours. Product development does require an investment, though.

- Equity in clients' businesses – If you work with startups or, perhaps, small businesses that have limited funds to pay you for your services, you could discuss payment by earning equity in their businesses. Your eventual payment might result from dividends, a buy-out by the founders or a cash-out if the clients' companies are sold or go public with their stock. Be sure to perform your due diligence before entering into arrangements like this. You might want to consult an attorney or business advisor to ensure that the contracts protect your rights and present the right deals.

In every way that you work to diversify your income, always consider the potential market for those efforts and how you will be able to market to your target audiences. Also, ask plenty of questions before you experiment with diversification activities. How well do diversification efforts align with your business model and mission? What types of indirect opportunities might arise as a result of you marketing new services? These and other questions will help you focus on the most promising ways to diversify your business and revenue, as well as how to effectively market them.

22
Marketing Remote Services

It seems that nearly every type of service can be marketed as and provided on a remote basis. Of course, certain elements of consulting, training, coaching, project management, technical services, product design work, etc. must be conducted on-site due to the required facilities or level of interaction necessary. However, I've have seen a transition from a high percentage of contract work being conducted on-site to the current trend towards remote, on-demand and outsourced contract services.

I've marketed my remotely delivered services to clients for nearly all of my career. Sometimes it seemed odd to me that I hadn't met in person the majority of my clients across the U.S. and abroad. With the use of conference calls, video calls, online collaboration platforms, emails and text messaging, shared cloud storage of files, and other communication and collaboration tools, it is easier than ever to work remotely.

Depending upon your industry and types of services, your marketing information might need to address how you overcome the challenges associated with working remotely. The key is to overcome any objections right from the start. Here are some issues I've experienced and solutions that have helped me prevent or address issues:

- Team inclusiveness – Physical proximity makes teamwork easier, due to opportunities for spontaneous conversations, the immediacy of sharing products or materials, ease in coordinating ad hoc meetings, and other advantages. When you're not present with your team, you just don't have the same level of participation and interaction as other team members. This can lead to not being up-to-date about developments, decisions, issues and nuances about the progress of projects. Sometimes these things don't come up during calls or other communications.

The best way I've found to stay connected with teams is to regularly communicate one-on-one with multiple team members. I ask plenty of questions, including ones such as, "Is there anything else I should know regarding the team or this project?" Typical status reports or exchanges tend not to cover what's going on behind the scenes. I try to initiate opportunities for less structured conversations for bond-building communication, like what might occur spontaneously in an office.

- Feedback about projects – It can be common to feel like you're working blindly at times as the remote worker. You might submit a report, parts of the project or other deliverables and receive inadequate feedback or even silence. This really depends on how responsive the client's project managers or teams are during the life cycle of the projects as well as how accustomed they are to working with remote professionals.

    The solution I've suggested to address this is that I'll directly ask for feedback when necessary, sometimes on a very specific level. For example, instead of just asking, "What do you think about this deliverable?" I might ask, "Have I missed anything?" and "Do you have suggestions to improve this deliverable?" If these types of questions don't elicit the responses I need, I'll identify very specific elements of the work and ask for notes or line item level changes. When all else fails, I'll call clients to review a document together or analyze the project step-by-step.

- Information security – Some projects involve proprietary content or sensitive information covered by non-disclosure agreements. These warrant security concerns. This can be a major issue with companies and some government agencies when working with contractors remotely. I've had projects in which written materials and messages couldn't be exchanged by email or an unsecured platform.

  I let prospects know that I use password protected or encrypted storage of files on my computers and backup systems. When security issues arose, I've explained what I could and couldn't provide to protect data and communications. My clients always have been helpful in providing direction on what I needed to do. So, the solution was to be up-front and honest about my capabilities.

It's a good idea to clearly state whether you work only remotely or are willing to work on-site when you market your services. With local clients, I mention that I am available for occasional on-site meetings and work sessions. It's been rare that out-of-town clients have wanted to incur the travel expenses for me to visit on-site during projects. I consider those requests on a case-by-case basis.

No matter where you prefer to perform your work, stress the benefits of your preference in your marketing materials. If there are particular issues or risks in your field, briefly explain how you resolve them in the marketing materials your prospects might see.

23
On-Call Services as a Package

There are significant benefits to offering on-call services as a package to clients. This contrasts with marketing your services to contract for single projects.

A big benefit of establishing on-call or on-demand contracts is having a steady stream of projects offered to you over long periods with clients who know and trust you. These arrangements are possible in most industries and apply to all types of services. That said, be aware that assignments can occur at inconvenient times, occasionally are high-pressure and may require a fair amount of resourcefulness due to the level of independence you're given.

An on-call relationship may be associated with an umbrella contract for your services over a given period for a set hourly rate. Frequently, on-call arrangements are just initiated on an understanding between you and a manager at a company. You're informally positioned and valued as the client's go-to, first-choice service provider. This is an ongoing relationship, with your rates potentially varying according to the services provided or nature of the projects.

I've been fortunate to have had numerous on-call service relationships in my career. Many spanned several years while a couple thrived for 12 years or more. Most of these clients initially engaged me for only one or two of my services. Over time, additional services were requested. I learned some skills on-the-job or via self-directed training. There were periods of full-time work as well as many gaps.

Additionally, I was hired a few times as what's called a sole-source on-call contractor. This was a fast-track hiring process for single, large projects that required significant subject knowledge and experience with an organization.

How do you address the challenge of marketing, finding and establishing on-call arrangements? Government on-call contracts typically are offered by request for proposals (RFPs) or by sole-source contracts that bypass standard RFP procedures. Placement agencies also might have on-call contracting opportunities offered only to a pre-arranged pool of contractors. Often, such arrangements are for projects with total costs under a set dollar threshold. These tend to be awarded to contractors with whom the staff previously worked, by referrals or through visibility among staff members via outreach, conferences or other connections.

Private sector businesses occasionally advertise such arrangements but more often than not, they evolve from a successful single project that turns into a series of assignments. The same is true with non-profit entities, when one project leads to many. Again, these arrangements frequently arise via referrals and some type of previous contact with managers and employees. Because on-call contracting opportunities may not be formal arrangements or advertised, your search for them must be ongoing, through networking and by building relationships.

What contractor performance tends to lead to on-call arrangements? The keys to establishing successful long-term, on-call arrangements are the same as for building any solid portfolio of clients. Here are some traits that my clients have said they look for:

- Solid experience and proven skills delivered on-time and on-budget, with competitive rates.

- Desire to learn about the client's business, including the industry, culture, challenges, processes and contracting procedures.
- Businesslike attitude and professional level business practices.
- Effective communication and collaboration skills.
- Clear and professional letters of agreement and project contracts.
- Willingness to drop everything at times for urgent projects. This can mean working some evenings and weekends, as necessary.
- Ability to perform with minimal supervision and direction.
- Resourcefulness and project management skills to get the job done despite challenges.
- Quality control to ensure work is done correctly the first time.
- Willingness to take the initiative to enhance skills or learn new ones based on client requests.
- Desire to provide exceptional service and go the extra mile to make clients look good and help their enterprises succeed.

Much of this is just about being professional in your dealings with prospects and clients. Your marketing can reflect this in many ways, by the content you present to your direct communications.

SMART MARKETING TIPS

24
Market to the Right Prospects

I've heard many associates repeat the mantra, "Any paying client is the right client." However, I suggest you focus on the types of prospective clients you want to work with for the projects that align with your long-term goals. This affords you the opportunity to target a defined group of prospects in marketing efforts to minimize the massive time and effort sinkhole when trying to get "just any" business.

Think about how you'd describe your ideal clients or customers. Factors could include the size of the business, the industry or sector they're in, the types of products or services they sell, your past relationship with staff members, the organization's culture, the size of budgets they have for your services, or even their location (e.g., local businesses offering face-to-face contact).

The right clients also can be the best ones to target strategically. By this I mean identifying certain prospects that, if successfully engaged for projects, can open doors in related areas. For example, an associate of mine who is an author, consultant and speaker has used strategic marketing to reach his ideal prospects—to get on their radar and have credibility with them. He spoke at relatively small conferences to build his credentials to be able speak at larger industry events. His strategy was to get in front of audiences that included executives at companies he wanted to target for specialized speaking events and consulting.

Although his keynotes became a significant revenue source over time, his paid workshop and training-type speaking at companies and non-profits cleared the way for consulting contracts. He felt that these audiences would be the best way to achieve his mission of moving an industry in a better direction when it came to certain business practices.

I know associates who cleverly marketed their experience working in industries to get highly targeted consulting engagements. Specifically, they focused on engaging with multinational companies to position themselves for international consulting, training or speaking opportunities. For a few associates, this was to establish a way for their work to support their love of travel. With some easy research, they identified companies that had major offices in the countries they wanted to visit. A strategy to facilitate this was to start by working with these companies' local or regional offices. This way, they had the right contacts to approach and could establish credibility with those organizations. It was an easy transition to then pitch their services internationally to these clients.

You always can expand your marketing efforts to additional prospects later, even some who are in the margins of the types you want to work with. This is on top of seizing opportunities to pitch prospects who come to your attention or approach you by referrals, industry visibility or through other means.

No matter what the stage of your business development, why not choose the people and organizations with whom you work? That's one of the big advantages of being in business for yourself. Your goal should be to only work with clients who align with your mission and business goals.

25
Target the Right Types of Projects

Perhaps you've heard the mantra, "Go after every type of project and take what you can get." I think it's a marketing approach that's adopted far too many times by self-employed businesspeople. I don't understand why. Not only does it sound like they're working from a position of desperation, which can have negative consequences, but it isn't a sound marketing strategy.

Way too much time will be spent seeking one-off, often low-budget projects that may not even align with the clients and industries you want to work with. It's how many "gig" workers operate. They focus on the volume of projects—also referred to as churning projects—to try to make a living. Long hours, as in working seven days a week and evenings, and low wages just isn't a sustainable business model. Quality that's just good enough is okay with many of them and even a great number of their clients.

What are the right types of projects to build a long-term, profitable business? One target is clients who clearly offer the potential for multiple projects. These are clients whom you've identified as having ongoing needs for your services. You research these prospects to ensure that they fit your criteria for desirable clients by their industry, work they do related to your services, pain points for which you have solutions and the type of cultures or people you'd like to engage with. Your goals should be to strategically and persistently find ways to build relationships with these prospects.

Once you have the opportunity to work with them on a project, you'll have proven your value as a go-to professional on an ongoing basis.

Depending upon the industry and your type of services, there may be a chance to set up a retainer-based arrangement or on-call contract. Otherwise, do what you can to remain visible to them over time to be offered projects as they arise—as a preferred service provider.

This has been the foundation of my business. I have one client for whom I've been an on-call consultant for over 20 years. I was an established contractor on-call for another client for about 13 years. Other businesses have been my clients for three years or more. These all started with one project or a set of needs. I periodically expressed my interest in being considered for more projects as they arose. I also made sure they knew about my full range of services.

Another important ingredient for business success is to pursue long-term projects. Clients with these projects offer efforts that range from weeks to months and, occasionally, years. You basically use the same strategy as with repeat clients. However, you target prospects you've researched to know they have lengthy projects or extended contractual engagements. This is no guarantee that you'll identify such prospects easily, so using the repeat client strategy is best. Then, you make it known that you're open to long-term projects and willing to commit to those by adapting your business as is necessary.

Long and time-intensive projects do mean that you're serving fewer clients and assuming a certain amount of risk by becoming somewhat dependent upon fewer contracts. You must weigh the pros and cons, as well as make a special effort to protect yourself if those long-term contracts end, expectedly or unexpectedly.

I've had long-term contracts and non-contractual commitments for a variety of my services. For some, I set a length of time for my commitment such as one year to establish the work activity or take the project to a certain point. One of my non-contractual projects—based on an understanding between the client and me—recurred for about two months every year, so I planned other work around it. I tend to have quite a few big, complex projects that vary from part-time to full-time for periods over several to many months. I've positioned myself with certain companies to be available for these contracts. However, they can occur at any time with little advance notice so there can be some scheduling challenges to resolve.

What about high-paying projects? These fall into the subcategory of dream clients we all hope to have, for repeat or long-term projects. From my experience, these are successful businesses or businesspeople who are willing to pay top rates for extraordinary service, quality of work and a high level of expertise.

I've only engaged with this type of client through referrals, as these projects are rarely advertised. As professionals gain years of experience, they're especially suited to be candidates for high-paying projects due to top-level skills and strong business connections. Always be on the lookout for prospects who appear to fit this category and devise strategies to position yourself for work opportunities.

26
Niche Services to Penetrate Markets

An effective way to establish a market position and build your business is to experiment with your marketing efforts by focusing on niches. This means you pitch certain services or skills to specific target markets. It's in contrast to marketing as a generalist in your field, reaching out to all possible desired types of potential clients.

I'm not saying that you should concentrate your long-term efforts on marketing only one skill or going after a very narrow group of clients. I'm advocating for an overall marketing strategy that includes experimentation with niches to test opportunities. These might be niches ignored by your competition or ones that you can dominate due to a highly customized approach. Ultimately, you'd aim to build visible and profitable positions within several niches. This would be a component of your marketing plan while still offering a variety of services to a reasonably broad market to ensure diversification.

Let's say that you're a programmer who develops Web sites. You can develop just about any type of site for any type of client using the most popular programming languages. That's just like thousands of other developers around the world. You can market your services to everyone you can reach, but that isn't very efficient. It's like randomly sending out a boilerplate email to 1,000 companies across the country and hoping for a one percent response rate.

Instead, what if you take a niche approach? First, you consider the types of Web sites you prefer building, the knowledge you have about particular industries, your credibility with a category of businesses and other characteristics that set you apart from other programmers. Then, you focus your marketing efforts on one or two niches associated with the following:

- A specific industry or audience with which you have a connection.
- Prospects in need of programming in a specific language or on a special platform.
- Sites designed for a specific purpose, such as sales, education, news or outreach.
- The type of site content, such as ones that are media-rich, interactive or multi-language.
- Site re-designs or upgrades.
- Prospects in a single location, such as locally, regionally or in a particular country.
- Sites that feature a certain design style.

Another niche approach is to focus on your own demographic. Use your own experience and insider knowledge to identify ways to target clients your age, education level, living situation, lifestyle, business sector, etc. After all, you might share certain business values, work situations, industry views and interests. A slightly different entry point is to look for products and services that cater to your demographic. Then, market to the companies that offer those products and services. You tailor your services to their needs related to serving people in your demographic. This idea could be developed many ways as a specialty.

If one niche doesn't work out, you move on to others. The goal is to experiment to find niches—pain points that you can address in selected markets—that yield the number and type of clients you want to have for the projects you want to do. These are called "verticals" as you're building depth in one or a few defined areas. At the same time, you remain open to general work that comes your way. That allows you to be diversified and maintain steady revenues to experiment with new niches.

I warn my associates about becoming overly dependent on single niches. It's like only knowing how to use one software tool. If something dramatically changes in the customer's market and it's no longer the tool in-demand, you suddenly could be left with no clients. Niches typically come and go, so it's wise to always be on the hunt for new ones.

It's also a good idea to look for niches outside your comfort zone. Also, look beyond your obvious client market based on your experience or connections. This allows you to explore new types of opportunities and pushes you to build on your skills and knowledge.

Ask yourself question like the following: What are your transferable skills? Which categories of new clients might need those skills and value the perspective you offer when considering your previous work? How can you re-frame your skills and knowledge to appeal to specific new audiences?

I encourage you to experiment with skill and market niches. Depth from a focus on verticals along with diversification in other areas of interest are the foundation of a sustainable and profitable solo venture or microbusiness.

27
Scaling Your Business for Opportunities

There are several ways to scale your business to expand your marketing opportunities: alliances, joint ventures, partnerships, subcontracting and co-ops.

You can do this to strategically increase your service offerings, enhance your credibility to target markets, propose strong teams for contract opportunities, pursue special ventures due to shared interests and create businesses to market-test specific services or products. Based on your experience working with others and the type of business you're in, you likely know which options fit best your work-styles and the opportunities you seek.

I've used all of the following scaling methods as part of my marketing strategy, except participation in a co-op. The results have been mixed. Here's a summary and my lessons learned for each:

- Alliances and joint ventures – I teamed with other professionals to pitch prospective clients or for RFP pitches. Projects ranged from consulting and research to media production and communication services. We had reasonable success winning contracts and the alliances definitely made us more competitive than if we had pitched ourselves alone. A big advantage was that this was a temporary arrangement, not a formal partnership, so we retained our independence.

    One lesson learned was how this is a great way to test working relationships with other professionals connected with my field. It was a good practice to establish a simple letter of agreement covering key business relationship points. The only negatives I experienced were some miscommunications during the proposal development and occasional creative differences during projects. Generally speaking, this has increasingly become my preferred way to scale my business over the years.

- Partnerships – I've formed a few partnership-based companies. These included corporations and LLCs. The purpose always was to combine our complementary skills, knowledge and contacts to provide services or create products that would be challenging to produce on our own. A couple of these could have been set up by subcontracting certain functions to specialists but joint ownership was part of the plan.

  Positive aspects included shared responsibilities, being on a team, frequent interactions and idea exchanges, a focus on work activities we preferred, shared risk, increased output and some operational cost savings. The most frequent negatives were disagreements on the direction to take with projects, divergence regarding long-term goals, prioritizing expenditures, management of creative differences and issues involving communication that resulted in interpersonal friction that negatively affected the businesses.

  Lessons learned? Think long and hard before forming partnerships to ensure that you and your partner(s) are on the same page regarding functional responsibilities, long-term goals, resolution of disagreements, decision-making processes and work-style compatibility. Many problems can be prevented by developing a good business plan. Also, take care in becoming partners with friends. While there are many advantages regarding trust and knowledge about each other, there are potential risks to those friendships if things go wrong with the venture. If your friendship is more important than the business, it might be better not to pursue a partnership together.

- Subcontracting – I've subcontracted a great many functions that I didn't have time for or that required special skills or equipment from professionals in other fields. In proposals and pitches, it was advantageous to be able to identify the highly qualified subcontractors I'd be teaming with on the projects.

    My experience subcontracting has been great. Over time, you can identify a set of go-to pros for various needs and have confidence that the jobs will be done correctly, efficiently, on-time, on-budget and often exceeding your expectations. The main lesson learned here is to take good care of subcontractors and they'll take good care of you. This includes paying them well and on time, as well as respecting their ideas and judgement. It's also important to establish clear, detailed letters of agreements to keep things transparent.

- Co-ops – I've interviewed with a couple of co-ops to consider participation. These were close-knit groups of professionals with complementary skills that tended to pursue narrow target markets such as non-profits or small businesses. I learned that business models vary for co-ops. Some are loosely tied solopreneurs, while others have formal expense and income sharing arrangements.

    The co-ops I checked out just weren't a good fit due to their narrow clientele emphasis and the partnership type structure. If you like the idea of being a part of a business work-sharing or marketing group, a co-op may be worth considering.

28
Referrals and Inside Tracks

Too many self-employed professionals underestimate the value of their industry contact networks. Also, they may not understand how to leverage those contacts to accelerate business growth through marketing.

Contact networks are assets that take some time to build. They're your trusted relationships formed through collaboration, work, school and other business connections. Your contacts often are or know the right people to pitch your services. That's gold when marketing your business.

I've used everything from spreadsheets to contact management software to organize my network for marketing efforts. I include all of their standard contact information, including **URLs** for their social network profiles. It also has been helpful to add reminders of projects we worked on or our business dealings, notes about people they might know who are relevant for my business and even conversation topics to use in future communications. I track the dates, methods of contact, and conversation or message exchange notes in this system.

There's an important lesson I've learned about maintaining a productive and growing network. It's the value of having conversations and brief message exchanges rather than launching into sales type interactions with my contacts. As natural occasions arise to ask for referrals and contract opportunities they're aware of, you seize those. You also can steer conversations in directions to create openings to ask about referrals and contracts. That said, there may be contacts you know so well that you can make such requests right off. Your long-term or close relationships may give you an edge due to timing, inside information as well as personal endorsements. We trust people whom our close contacts trust. And referrals from our contacts are carry positive weight in decisionmaking.

My one rule in relationships with my contact network is to initially focus on finding ways to help them in some way. The favor is nearly always returned, very often as direct offers to connect me with prospective clients or business opportunities. For example, I might send a contact a referral, resource, informative article or business lead. Their thank-you notes very often include an invitation for them to reciprocate. I rarely would ask for anything right away with a new contact, but I do follow up with requests when appropriate occasions arise. This mutual assistance strategy pays off and is a sustainable marketing strategy.

When looking for referrals for contracting opportunities or connections to contacts, the more specific you are about what you're interested in the better. One of my associates was having little success getting contact referrals from former clients. He offered a wide range of online marketing services and asked for referrals who needed any of those services and in any industry. I suggested that an approach might be to focus specifically on one or two of the hottest services—likely common pain points for prospects—and one industry that might be ignored by his competition. This is niche marketing. It helps contacts narrow down possible referrals right from the start.

One of your primary marketing efforts should be to seek referrals to connect with potential clients and find inside tracks to identify available contracts. It's the hidden business opportunity market—similar to the hidden job market—and it's available to you through your contact network.

29
Prospect Research to Increase Pitch and Proposal Success

Far too many professionals waste marketing time and effort pursuing the wrong clients and submitting ineffective pitches. Sometimes it's laziness and other times it's due to a lack of confidence in their research skills.

To be clear, the wrong clients are ones who likely don't use your types of services or aren't a good fit for you. Ineffective pitches are boilerplates that focus only on you and not enough of the prospects' needs. That is, how you have solutions for the specific types of needs or problems they face now and in the future.

The only way to increase your chances for success is to identify which prospects to pitch or offer proposals. Then, find ways to customize your content by investing the time to research answers to key questions.

Begin with questions to uncover the information critical for your decision about whether to pitch the prospects. Your goal is to identify prospective clients you can and want to serve for the long-term, a key for your business to be sustainable. For example, consider the following questions:

- What would you say if a prospective client asked you what you know about the company? (Being specific, beyond generalities about what they do, how big they are, where they're located, etc.)

- How would you describe the prospect's market position, for their products or services, in a way that shows you understand their business?
- What are your impressions of the prospect's products or services?
- What are the prospect's vision and values?
- What sets this prospect apart from their competition and other organizations in general?
- How does this prospect align, in business model and performance, with industry trends?
- What is it about the prospect's communications in blogs, Web content and interviews that make them sound authentic and meaningful?
- How do the needs of this prospect align with work you wish to do in the short-term or long-term?
- Why might you feel invested in the success of this prospect over time?
- Why do the leaders and staff connected with your area of work seem like individuals with whom you'd like to work?

The following are my favorite sources to reveal answers to questions like those stated above:

Prospect's Web site – Review their product or service marketing information, leadership profiles, case studies, blog, news releases, current white papers or reports, career page, and "About us" or company overview content.

LinkedIn – Check the prospect's page for overview information, posts and articles, leaders and employees to whom you are connected as well as profiles to look up. Check out "Similar companies" to know their competition, the "See jobs" page for employment needs trends and any available Slideshare decks to view their presentations.

Glassdoor – Survey the overview, employee reviews, photos, interviews, updates, awards and jobs for their employment needs and trends. Use your judgement about the quality of the information provided, because many rating sites like this tend to show more negatives than positives.

Industry and financial publications – Read articles by and about the prospect, quotes from leaders and employees, the most current articles about the prospect's industry and trends, and assessments about the prospect's financial performance.

This approach to research on prospective clients should get you off to a good start selecting better prospects and developing far better pitches or proposals. That way, you'll avoid the frustration of wasting time and effort in your marketing efforts.

As you gain experience conducting this type of research, you'll identify the most productive ways to uncover valuable details and shortcuts depending on your industry. Use research to give yourself a competitive advantage in your marketing and impress prospective clients with your insights about them.

30
Pitching Your Services at Interviews

What's your story about your services and how you can solve clients' problems? What will they gain from hiring you? Can you tell your story in a way that engages prospects and is meaningful from their perspective (not just yours)?

Many people who are new to self-employment haven't developed the skills to tell these stories effectively or comfortably. This is person-to-person sales and a key component of overall marketing efforts. We may not like the sales aspects of self-employment but our ability to handle this role likely will be the difference between success and failure in our ventures.

I believe that preparation is the key to feeling confident about pitching my services. In other words, I start by knowing my audience, anticipating their questions and being crystal clear about how my specific services can solve their problems. Then I'm prepared to open a conversation with them that leads to further discussion or being hired.

For example, I was contacted about a project by a company for which I had worked a couple years prior. I met this new project manager via a phone call. She described the project and asked me to come to her office to discuss it and my services. In advance, I conducted some research on their client and the subject matter.

During the interview, she asked me if the project seemed like a good fit. I described my experience with a similar project, including how I addressed some challenges my team faced. I mentioned several points that showed I knew about her customer's operations related to the project as well as some pain points our end product could address. After that, I suggested a few ideas on how we could handle this specific project.

My final thoughts included the fact that I worked as a contractor with her company previously and what my rates were for these types of services. That seemed to cover everything she wanted to discuss. I took that opportunity to ask her some questions about the customer's team, special aspects with this project, the level of creative freedom we'd have, our team members and the set-up for our contract.

This approach is quite different than how many contractors just focus on "selling" their experience and skills. Too often, they talk only about themselves rather than about the prospective clients and their needs. I've had far more success pitching clients when I concentrated on their pain points through the lens of my experience, skills and services.

In this example, I began by assuring her I was qualified for this project and that I was experienced in solving problems typical for such projects. I made it clear that I was knowledgeable about her customer and sensitive to issues that might arise. This implied that I appreciated the importance of this project to them.

To reflect my interest in this work, I provided some initial ideas regarding our collaboration on aspects specific to this project. I also casually reminded her of my previous contracts with her company and established my current rate. Finally, by asking her several questions, I proactively shifted the conversation to our business relationship.

What I was doing was answering my prospective client's questions in advance of her actually having to ask them. She gave me the opportunity to do this easily by her general opening question.

What if this were a general interview where you'd be pitching a variety of services? I'd suggest that all of your preparation be shifted to her company and the types of projects you'd likely be hired to handle. You might describe how you've previously worked with some of her clients, if that's the case.

Also, you might focus on recent projects they handled and pain points you think they might be facing. You'd want to make clear connections between their needs and how your skills, knowledge and experience would apply to them. Again, the pitch would be about her company and its needs within the context of how your services would be beneficial to them.

31
Customer Service as a Marketing Tactic

Outstanding customer service should be a big part of your marketing efforts. Chances are that your experience has taught you to provide top notch services, be very responsive in work and communications, complete projects on time and on budget, and follow through on promises to build lasting and profitable relationships.

For anyone who provides great customer service, it's not unusual for clients to informally request additional services. In these cases, you must determine if it's appropriate to provide the services or if this is an indication of project scope creep. You must decide whether the new task should be a legitimate line item added to the scope of work or part of your customer service marketing strategy. Unless I want to absorb the cost of these services as a worthwhile investment in the relationships, I discuss the work changes with my clients in a positive manner.

A marketing mindset supports doing small favors for clients whether those activities are related to the project for which we've been hired or even a bit outside the project. However, cases of obvious scope creep must be controlled by discussing the change order to the contract when the services are requested.

In addition to offering a high level of customer service to clients on projects, I often employ a type of marketing that has successfully grown profitable ongoing relationships after projects have been completed. For example, when I run across an article that may be of interest to a client, I'll forward that with a brief note explaining why I thought it was relevant. This note might read something like, "I thought of you and your work involving [fill in the topic] when I read this article. I look forward to working with you on another project soon." Sometimes I'll connect my services to the article by saying, "This article is about [fill in the topic] and I thought you'd find it informative. I may not have mentioned that I also provide [fill in the type of service at least somewhat related to the article] in addition to how I contributed to our previous collaboration."

Outstanding customer service gives you the opportunity to prompt clients to remember that you did a great job on a project—often called relationship marketing. They'll recall that it was nice to work with you as well as how you went above and beyond along the way. You want to be that memorable contractor who remains on the client's radar for future work.

What is the right level of customer service for you? Only you can decide. It's a balancing act sometimes. Much of the decision about limits revolves around how well a client treats you, as relationships are a two-way street. If you're treated very well by a client, it feels natural to treat them well. Good clients understand that your time and expertise costs them money. Just be careful not to be taken advantage of or sacrifice earned income by being the overly generous person you probably are.

32
Conversations With a Touch of Marketing

A business friend exclaimed the other day, "Who talks anymore? And why would I spend time talking without a very specific agenda?" That's a problem on many levels because those are rarely conversations that build relationships. Plus, they tend to eliminate the chance to stumble upon unexpected opportunities.

Nearly all of my associates have adopted text messaging, emails, social network messaging and video calls to quickly say what they want to say or ask questions. Electronic communication is efficient. It's my primary tool for interaction with clients, associates and prospects. This level of communication gets business done.

Yet, a handful of holdouts among my associates and I openly admit to preferring calls and face-to-face meet-ups to have less structured conversations when possible. Each week, I try to make sure that I have at least a couple of unstructured conversations that flow spontaneously in various directions within and outside our particular industries or professions. We ask each other questions and share thoughts about issues we're facing and ideas we've come across. Often, we discuss projects we're working on to get each other's insights. It's not uncommon to mention opportunities we've spotted, as well.

The best way to be comfortable conversing is just to start doing it and remember how to listen more than talk. Look for reasons to connect people you know with things you read, see, hear about, do and think about—all are excuses to talk.

I'm convinced that you will be at a disadvantage professionally by not having unstructured business conversations. There are big benefits to these meaningful exchanges. Conversations help build relationships beyond narrow business transactions. Also, they help uncover trends, reveal new connections among business ideas, present the chance to have our assumptions and actions questioned, and offer compelling topics to explore. We often discover shared interests and even ideas to collaborate on. Conversations aid in networking and in marketing to identify new opportunities. To not enjoy these benefits is a serious disadvantage in business.

I've unexpectedly obtained referrals to new clients and was alerted about projects via conversations. Some informal chats have prompted me to change directions on business decisions, saving me time and effort due to erroneous conclusions I had made. I've been introduced to people I might never have met if not for a single idea discussed in passing and someone saying, "I should introduce you to one of my contacts who'd enjoy talking with you about this subject."

If you're uncomfortable starting conversations, here are a few openers I often use:

- I came across this article on [fill in the topic] and wondered what you think about it.
- We haven't connected in quite a while, what interesting projects are you working on these days?
- I'm working on a project dealing with [fill in the description] and I'm curious to get your thoughts.

Conversations put humanness back into our business lives and as part of our marketing communications. We get to know what and how others think about business topics, what they're curious about and insights they've built on their knowledge and experience. Some of this comes down to having empathy for others. Also, conversations build trust, long-term business relationships and valuable communication channels that can be especially helpful for us due to the challenges we face as solopreneurs and microbusiness professionals.

So, learn to talk with—not just talk to—others to reap the many benefits. Set aside a half-hour or an hour to converse with a colleague or business contact each week. Ask questions. Explore what's on each other's minds. Listen, learn, be inspired and feel connected.

33
Leveraging Client Interactions to Expand Services

Meetings, collaborations, check-ins and guidance chats on the fringes or outside your scope of work can be huge schedule busters. However, they can be marketing opportunities. That this, ways to expand your services to those clients. The key is to prevent these communications from forcing you to exceed time estimates you set in proposals and end up decreasing hours available to perform the core work of the contract.

I've been asked to participate in more conference calls and meetings ever since I was deemed "senior level" in my profession. I also receive far more calls from project managers during contract work, often to provide consulting on business at the edges of or outside the contracts' scopes of work. With conference calls and meetings, I'm asked to listen in for my take on what's happening internally with projects or to provide my outsider's perspective. Project managers frame this as wanting to keep me up to date on aspects of the projects. They also ask for my thoughts on planning, trends related to the projects or input on other activities.

To make this work out fairly for my clients and for me, I've learned to be strategic in providing these extra services. First, I set the stage initially to control scope creep by addressing this issue specifically at the contract development stage. This is when I estimate the hours or flat fee for a project. I ask about the number of meetings and calls planned, but also estimate the number of additional ones based on similar projects. Additionally, I try to nail down the frequency and duration of status or check-in calls, collaboration calls, and other discussions.

In the media production industry, the unknowns about projects fall into what's commonly called a contingency budget. All contract professionals should consider adding such a line item or basing estimated costs for client communication, meetings and other interactions on worst case scenarios. At a minimum, consider including a note in agreements about how this issue will be handled. I state that if interaction hours are trending above estimates due to the addition of consultations or other interactions, a change order for our contract may be required. This is to ensure that budgets for other aspects of the project aren't negatively affected. It also makes it easier for me to control what I do on-the-clock and as a relationship building service.

When I invest some extra time in client interactions I so do as a marketing tactic to build trust, broader communication and reinforce my client's perception of my professional value. This can be a chance to show that I can provide additional services beyond our original contract. In other words, I might participate in extra meetings or collaborations to offer guidance knowing that I'll eventually mention how those services can continue after the current project is completed.

Timing is everything in this case. I wait for opportunities in conversations or message exchanges to softly pitch my additional services carefully tailored to the client's needs. I avoid using sales language or make it sound like I've been doing them a favor up to this point by not charging for my time. It's better to bring up the services framed in a way that makes them sound more formal or packaged to contrast with the informality of what has happened thus far.

The key is to offer soft up-selling messages when it seems that there's a need due to requests for extra assistance or there has been scope creep. It seems easier to have the conversations this way and there's a better chance that your existing contract will be amended to continue your work with the clients.

34
Hidden and Subtle Marketing Opportunities

A key to smart marketing is identifying and acting on opportunities that your competition doesn't look for or see. Your industry knowledge and experience position you to know where and how to spot signs that prospective clients need your assistance.

The challenge is that it's easiest to seek the low hanging fruit type opportunities that arise through ads, referrals and other conventional means. It's more complicated to use detective work to reveal hidden opportunities using business-social networks, contacts' blogs and news sources.

The following are some methods my associates and I have used to spot and respond to opportunities. The objective is to cultivate relationships with potential clients by starting conversations. Ideally, these exchanges lead to you to pitch your services for needs they identify. You'll only see these opportunities by regularly scanning posts, blogs and news on your social network platforms and by receiving news or reports from relevant industry sources. Note that my reference to social networks means your direct connections as well as contacts through professional interest groups with members who could be potential clients. Note that you must be searching outside communication channels populated only by colleagues in your profession.

I suggest that you start by looking for the following opportunities:

- Requests for referrals – You may find social network posts with requests for referrals by individuals looking to connect with service providers. Chances are that the posters wish to avoid advertising their needs to avoid mass responses and to fast-track their contracting. They trust that referred providers have been vetted by colleagues or contacts. One approach is to respond through private messaging with offers to discuss their needs and how your services might be what they're looking for. Be sure to cite a bit of information that shows you did some homework on the individual and/or company. You can mention that if your services aren't a good fit, you'll try to connect them with someone you know and trust. Little favors build relationships.

- Clearly expressed needs for contract work candidates – You always want to respond to these notices or social network posts via private messages or email. Include details about why your services are a good fit as well as some content that shows you know something about the individual's business. This is a very brief and personalized pitch. You are much more likely to get a response if you make this small effort, than by only forwarding your email address or phone number along with the message, "Contact me" or "I'm interested."

- Implied needs for services – What content in a social network post implies a need for services? An example would be a post that describes an issue a person or business is facing, along with questions or requests for suggestions. This is a chance to provide useful feedback with an offer to discuss it more. That's when you'd mention your services, not as an aggressive sales pitch but as part of the conversation.

- News about rapid company growth – Rapid growth often results in urgent needs for specialized talent, with contract services being the fastest solution. Use contacts or research to identify the right person to approach. Then, customize your pitch by referring to the specific needs you interpret that they have and your qualifications to help. Frame your pitch around your value during their rapid growth.

- Announcements about launches of startups – Essentially, you would use the same approach as with rapidly growing companies. The difference is that the founders might feel that they cannot afford your services. Also, they might think you won't understand their particular startup culture. You must specifically address these hurdles. For example, say that you're open to creative payment arrangements such as a scaled rate plan or equity. Cite your previous experience working successfully with startups. Reduce their doubts right off.

- News about or by companies of interest – By offering substantive comments regarding the posted news, you become visible to those other readers and the companies. You might be able to identify company contacts in the news to approach or start an exchange based on their responses to your comments. From my experience, comments that get noticed include recommended resources related to their news, solutions regarding their challenges or offers to connect them with your contacts.

- Posts about promotions of people working in your field – Use messages to congratulate contacts as excuses to start exchanges or conversations. That allows to you mention how your services might be of interest to them later. Use conversations to inquire about their work and businesses to identify pain points.

Always emphasize conversations more than sales, customize pitches citing specific needs and make it personal to foster relationships. Listen, ask questions and seek engagement to turn subtle online opportunities into new business.

35
Proposing New Project Ideas to Clients

Your marketing messaging may include how, as an outsider, you offer fresh ideas and assumption challenging advice on projects. So, you might have certain expectations about how open clients will be to your thinking when you're hired. They should be receptive when it comes to the work you've been hired to do. But how might they react if you think beyond the current project and propose a new project that you believe would be in their best interests?

As part of your ongoing marketing efforts with clients, it makes sense to propose project ideas to them at appropriate times and in appropriate ways. I've found clients to be most receptive to project ideas toward the end of the current projects. That way, we have the momentum and positive results established to bolster trust in the collaboration.

The best way to propose a project idea is as part of a conversation when there seems to be a natural opportunity. Concisely describe the problem or need you've identified while working with the client and how you could help with a solution. The tone would be something like that of a close advisor and team member making an informed suggestion.

If your client expresses interest, offer to write up a more detailed proposal. This is a new project so be prepared to spend a bit of time collaborating with your client on the details and your scope of work. There also might be an approval process required before you can launch the effort.

Unless you have a deep relationship with a client, I wouldn't propose more than one project at a time. Also, I'd be careful not to make your pitch sound purely like a sales offer. Think of it as being a part of your consulting services, part of the value you offer by providing an outside perspective on the current project and beyond.

36
Packaging Your Services

Online contractor-business platforms are driving a trend toward productization of a wide range of services. Essentially, this involves packaging and pricing an end product rather than charging by the hours to produce it. This is an emerging tactic that's affecting how many professionals market their services. The downside is that it can devalue experience, skill level and knowledge.

Here's how the online model works. These platforms sign up contractors as on-call providers. For example, their services might from content marketing and consulting to graphic design and executive coaching. Buyers purchase packages of these services for one-time flat fees or monthly flat fee subscriptions. The platform handles the marketing and fee collection. They pay service providers a flat fee and, in most cases, no matter how much time it takes to complete the projects.

To compete with these platforms and a growing marketplace that seems to prefer productization, some independent professionals are experimenting with the same model. For example, let's say you offer business plan consulting and development services. Traditionally, you'd prepare a proposal that's customized for the client based on discussions about their project. Your proposal would include a list of specific services tuned to their unique needs, time frames, your hourly rate and final deliverables.

The productization model changes this. A business plan "product" could be a flat fee for complete preparation of a 15-page plan. Interviews, research, writing and consulting would be built into this fee, determined by the average requirements of past projects like this. There still could be separate add-on packages for additional flat fees, such as an option for three hours of extra consulting or a 10-slide presentation deck for the plan.

The advantage for both parties is that this model is easy to understand and market due to it being focused on the end product. Everyone knows the cost, like buying a product off the shelf. Services that have been priced on an hourly basis now can be offered in a more transparent, but generic, way. Services become commodities.

A disadvantage is that those end products representing packages of services tend to be marketed more on price than on quality, customization, experience of the providers and provider-client relationships. Service providers must play a game of averages with the hours and resources necessary to deliver the end products while keeping the costs low enough to compete globally. This is a bit like converting a nuanced human-based service into a robotically or computer-based production model.

Often, this turns into a race to complete projects as quickly as possible to maximize profits versus a focus on quality, customer service and uniqueness of the work to support a brand. How do you convince prospective clients that your packaged service is worth more than the same product from an online platform costing less? Will they value your experience, knowledge and skills or focus on the product price?

If you wish to productize services that can fit this model, I suggest that you step into it incrementally. Some services can be packaged and marketed far more effectively than others. You don't want to be locked into a set pricing model that doesn't take into account the value you offer. You may find more success by carving out a niche that separates your work from "commodity" type work.

37
Options to Work With Cash-Strapped Clients

I think it would be safe to say the majority of professionals operate by an inflexible rule: "No pay, no play." In other words, prospective clients who don't have the funds to pay appropriate rates for services are not worthy of marketing outreach. They should wait until they do have funds before asking for business services. Yet, consider cases when this steadfast rule might be short-sighted.

If your cash-flow situation requires that you focus your time and effort only on paying clients, that's the right choice. You've got to pay the bills and be paid yourself. However, it might be a good idea to be open to alternative compensation when you have enough paying clients to cover overhead and some compensation. Why? Because there are arrangements that may pay off in other ways or in greater amounts in the long-run.

For example, "other ways" might include loyalty-based relationships, such as a contractual commitment to work with you at a certain point in their growth. The "greater amounts" I mentioned could be your accumulated fees, equity in the client's business, some type of commission-based compensation or monetary bonuses in some form. This may be an attractive option for professionals who have the business experience to make sound judgements in these cases.

Here's how I handled one of these cases. I was introduced to a cash-strapped prospective client via a referral from an associate. The company's team was authentic, passionate and had great products. I quickly learned that they needed the types of services I provided. We ended up establishing a contract with me being paid in company stock.

I did specify a limit to the amount of work I would provide over time, as I couldn't afford to over-commit to this type of speculative deal.

Without getting into the details, it worked out to be a fair arrangement all around. When the company is sold, taken public or when dividends are paid, the value of my investment in them likely will increase significantly. The income potential may be far higher than if I just received payment for my hours worked.

In addition to negotiating attractive equity payment agreements, you might consider deferred payment, contracts for future work, barter deals, commission-based contracts or other creative alternatives to direct payment. Sometimes contracts like these are very simple and relatively low risk. If you sense elevated risk or the dollar amounts could be quite high, it might be best to consult a business lawyer for guidance and to review the contracts. Be aware that any of these alternative payment arrangements could have tax and legal implications that must be researched prior to signing any agreements.

Deferred payment might involve logging your hours over the defined period so that the full amount can be paid at a prescribed date. You may want to charge a higher rate due to the delayed payment or set up a mutually agreed upon bonus to be added as compensation. A contract for future work is just that. The client agrees to hire you for a certain number of hours each month in the future or maybe put you on retainer starting when a certain revenue level is reached.

Barter deals work when your client has products or services you need that offer an equitable amount of value as that of your services. Commission-based contracts could involve you earning a percentage of the client's new business somehow tied to your work. There are other creative alternatives being used by solopreneurs and microbusinesses, including deals involving payment in cryptocurrencies.

Besides the equity arrangement with one company, I've employed deferred payment, future work and commission-based options a handful of times. There have been a few times when I wasn't paid the full amounts due for my work and only a couple have completely failed to pay. I typically have one or two of these alternative compensation arrangements active most years as "investments" to earn a larger return than just from my hourly or project rates. Most often, it's work with promising startups.

You never know what opportunities might arise from your marketing efforts. It's always a good idea to be open to all types of client relationships. Even though it sounds unconventional, a service provider could even focus specific marketing efforts to contract with cash-poor clients. If your risk is managed prudently, you could end up with some of your best clients and financial deals.

My warning about any alternative payment arrangement is that there are real risks of not getting paid or compensated for your work. Many things can go right and wrong, with the majority being out of your control. Only commit to an alternative arrangement after appropriate research, expert guidance and solid agreements or contracts.

38
Pitching Solutions to Prospects

In the process of marketing your services to prospects, there probably will be a point when you must pitch your solutions—the ideas you have to offer—in writing, verbally or in presentations.

I've pitched countless approaches and solutions to prospects over the years. I built sound business cases for the ideas I proposed and the majority of my ideas were well-received. However, when I wanted to push comfort zones with unconventional or highly creative ideas, I felt far more pressure to craft pitches that addressed the expected resistance. There was risk associated with pitching big ideas but also with the pitch development process itself.

Your professional experience in your field doesn't necessarily equip you to pitch big and maybe even disruptive level ideas as an outsider of an organization. Doing that as an employee can risk one's job, especially if given a go-ahead and the effort fails. Most businesspeople are conditioned to play it safe even when they know such an approach often leads to mediocrity and increased risk from competition.

Pitching what are sometimes big, business-changing ideas and approaches has been a critical element of my work. When I develop pitches like these, I initially focus on my audience and what their pain points are. I need to have a picture of how well they understand the pain point, what their concerns or fears are, what's at stake, what types of solutions they're accustomed to embracing and how the pain points are connected to other issues or functions in their business.

Additionally, I try to understand other background information that offers context for their pain points. This helps direct me toward the right content for my idea or approach and how to present my pitch.

It's always a good idea to try to hook your prospect's attention right from the start within the framework of a story. Their problem is the conflict that needs to be resolved. This means we're talking about touching emotions and setting the stage for an evidence-based argument supporting a set of actions to take. You do this because you need their attention and to get them to listen.

There are occasions when the only choice is to build a story around the risk or negative consequences of not effectively addressing the problem. My preferred angle is to focus on the benefits of using my proposed ideas or approaches—with the emphasis on positives.

For example, the opening of your pitch could be to entice a prospect to imagine a scenario in which their problem is resolved. Guide them to visualize your big idea or approach being successful. This is the impact on their operations, marketing or sales, industry position, or whatever area of their business would be affected most by the problem being eliminated. Then, move on to how this can be accomplished by a set of well thought-out, evidence-based and measurable steps.

Here are a few more tips on pitching ideas and approaches:

- Focus on the solution itself, not just on general benefits such as the monetary potential or "change the world" effect. What's the emotional, inspirational, memorable and meaningful core of this idea that will drive benefits and ultimately success?
- Use familiar terms, examples and concepts in the description of your solution or approach so it doesn't sound completely foreign to the audience.

- Frame and define the problem by identifying the underlying cause and build a logical argument to solve it.
- Support your commitment to establishing or maintaining the organization's superior market position, staying ahead of disruptive competition and supporting an innovation-centered culture.
- When defining the problem to be addressed, explain why it matters, what it means to solve it and what's needed to solve it efficiently and effectively.

With good preparation, you'll have addressed nearly all of your prospect's questions in your pitch or are prepared to answer them during a discussion.

How many details about your solution should you disclose in your pitch? In some cases, this depends on how close you are to getting a contract signed and your relationship with the prospect. I've rarely worried about a prospect using my solutions without hiring me. So much of success is in the execution of processes and adaptations as projects proceed, not just the solutions. Prospects are hiring us for the delivery of solutions, not just the magical sounding answers we offer.

39
Strategic Use of Content Marketing

Content marketing is a way to publish useful information, educational or training material, or advice online aimed at target audiences. The goal is to establish your expertise, build relationships and increase your business' visibility. It's often described as indirect marketing because you're not hard selling or using traditional advertising. You're offering something of value to establish connections that can lead to new business.

The best content is created from your experience and knowledge, rather than content re-published from others. This means you must learn to be comfortable using one or more of the common content marketing distribution methods. These include writing articles or books, producing your own podcasts or video-blogging.

Your original content is the most effective type of information because you can shape the messaging, ensure that it's authentic and communicate with your "voice" so audiences get to know you. It's a way to speak directly to prospective clients' interests and needs.

For example, your written content may take the form of short or long articles distributed or broadcasted on various publishing platforms. These include social networks, a blog on your Web site or a blogging platform, personal content platforms that serve as e-magazines or feature story platforms, Web sites that feature your column or articles, or other online platforms that serve as publishing and news mediums.

Podcasts can be distributed on your Web site, personal podcasting platforms or business themed platforms that feature collections of podcast series from various experts. Video blogs can be distributed on your Web site, general video platforms or business themed platforms that feature collections of video series from experts. Basically, this is a method of self-syndicating your content. Your writing or recordings should appear on channels that your target audiences see or hear.

Why should you consider using content marketing to build your business? Sharing your wisdom and expertise for free is an effective way to enhance your market position as an expert in your field. Content marketing works for many professional fields and within most industries. The results include incoming inquiries about your services, requests for interviews by reporters and bloggers, invitations to speak at events, and referrals by your audience members.

Your main investment with content marketing is your time. That's unless you need assistance to produce the content or you must pay for a presence on certain platforms. Yet, most of the well-known platforms for writing and media are free to use for distribution of content.

What type of content should you develop? The simple answer is to address the pain points of your target audience with solutions, insights, advice and resources from your knowledge and experience. Industry issues, trends and problems you've faced can be compelling content.

This might sound like you're giving away your services. However, the content you're distributing is not specific to companies, so you're really providing teasers or general suggestions for what you could do for audience members as clients. The strategy is to show them the high level of value you have to offer so they hire you for projects.

Your content must resonate with your audience. It should speak to them as it would if coming from a coach, trusted advisor, educator or industry expert. Personal stories, anecdotes and insights are readable, memorable and attract readers. Make your content presentation like a conversation, as it would be if the audience members were your clients already. Authenticity is critical. You're giving your audience the virtual experience of collaborating with you as their service provider.

40
Online Contract Applications

Online contract applications can be marketing minefields due to intentional or unintentional built-in bias. These can relate to experience, skills, knowledge, cost or industry-specific preconceptions. To help prevent exclusion, you must be strategic about the information and language you use in applications.

In a conversation I had with an associate about his experience with online contract applications, he brought up the same questions I've asked myself when crafting responses, such as:

1. If I describe my experience in detail, how do I prevent being considered underqualified or overqualified, cut-rate or too expensive, etc.?
2. If I've worked on projects that are only somewhat similar to the opportunity presented, will the contracting manager still see that my overall qualifications position me well for their project?
3. If I state my typical rate for a particular type of work and am not allowed to explain the value that represents, am I setting myself up to be uncompetitive with other applicants?
4. If I hold back on disclosing information that might trigger rejection of my applications, will contracting managers just gather that information on my social network profiles anyway?

There are no simple answers to these questions because each application, type of project and employer is different. And it's not like there's any standard review process or criteria for contractors across all industries. Every company handles contractor selection differently, using different online platforms and candidate management systems. There's no way to escape at least some degree of bias in this process.

I've found little value in trying to game online systems. Contracting managers and procurement staff often consider candidates differently than human resources and recruitment staff. Because contractors are hired for specific projects or defined time periods, there's more emphasis on the scope of services and desired outcomes.

There's also general acceptance by established companies that more experienced contractors charge more for their services. For example, a regionally known business keynote speaker might charge $8,000 but a nationally known one might command $20,000 or more due to fame and perceived value. Hiring 10 less qualified speakers at $2,000 each, like they might do in job hiring, just doesn't offer the same value as contracting with the top-level speaker.

What's the best approach when pitching your services via online applications? As much as possible, emphasize the value you have to offer. This means your qualifications and solutions for those particular prospects. It's all related to your experience and how you can blend that with relevant knowledge to solve problems that clients face today.

This may seem obvious but be sure to answer every question and provide everything asked for in online applications. You can't assume that you'll be given the chance to provide information later at an interview or another step of their process. Always be meticulous when filling out those online applications. Think through every piece of information you provide and the language you use as subtle or direct marketing messaging.

41
Marketing Your Services Through Agencies

There are thousands of staffing, placement, recruiting, temp agencies and other entities that connect contractors with organizations for work locally, regionally, nationally and internationally. An agency can be a worthwhile marketing partner, depending upon your field and market niche.

Many of my associates who provide contract technical writing, graphic design, e-learning production and software development services have had success finding work through agencies. Some have reported that their hourly rates were less than if contracting directly with clients, though. However, they point out that they likely wouldn't have had the opportunity to work with those clients if not for the agencies' relationships with the companies.

Many large companies and federal agencies used to directly hire the majority of their contractors. Due to the resources required to procure and manage a large number of contractors in many fields, they eventually switched to agencies to handle all contractor arrangements. Unfortunately, adding a middleman like this can be a disadvantage for independent professionals who prefer to contract directly with clients.

I've found two ways to address the agency-only challenge. One is to team with a larger business that already has an on-call or project contract with a company that rarely hires solopreneurs. For example, I've contracted with an e-learning program development firm that provides ongoing services to large corporations. Therefore, I was an on-call specialist sub-contractor for a business that didn't need to work through an agency.

Another way around the agency-only situation is to build a relationship with the project manager who uses your type of services. In some cases, you may be considered for special temporary contracts established outside the agency. Sometimes these engagements are considered "sole source" contracts due to the expertise needed or other characteristics of the project.

If you want to work through an agency to enhance your marketing, I suggest you find one that specializes in your field. Ideally, it should be positioned to place professionals like you with the types of projects you desire as well as with your hourly rate range. Definitely do some research to find an agency that's a good fit, including talking with a few solopreneurs who have worked with the agency. Be very clear about all fees and payment arrangements.

Also, I'd think long and hard about signing an exclusive agreement or one that limits in any way your rights to pursue work outside the agency's service. It would require an extraordinary guarantee of performance on their end to make an exclusive contract even worth considering. Understand that most agencies contractually obligate you to work through them with clients they connect you with. This is so you can't contract directly with their clients after they introduce you, as a way to avoid their fees.

An interesting development regarding marketing through agencies is that we're seeing increasingly frequent reports of talent shortages, changes in workforce hiring trends and more openness to remote and contract workers. This points to promising opportunities for agencies that place solopreneurs. Perhaps such matchmakers will be a more helpful component of our marketing strategies in the future.

42
Online Freelancing Platforms

A few years ago, I decided to start giving some online freelancing job platforms a try as a marketing experiment. I signed up with my business information and profile to be listed on around 10 of the most popular free platforms or ones where I received free credits to try out their services. I'd say that half of them covered nearly every type of job, ranging from management consulting and graphic design to dog walking and window cleaning. Others focused more on professional services for businesses and organizations.

What are my findings for this ongoing experiment? My records indicate that I've applied or submitted proposals for nearly 100 contract projects. Probably three-quarters of the projects were posted by individuals without obvious business entities identified. The balance of them were clearly posted by representatives of companies or organizations.

This effort has resulted in only a handful of contracts so far. Surprisingly, two were through platforms that are matchmakers for every type of service. Those were posted by individuals, not businesses. Several other contracts were via platforms strictly for business-to-business services.

A couple of projects were months-long and profitable with good clients—an individual and a large company. One little project was for a small business. Another project was for a new non-profit organization. For them, I decided to provide pro bono services and fee-based work later on. Interestingly, I was chosen for two projects after those clients had bad experiences with what they described as "lowest-cost service freelancers."

I suspect that I've been rejected for the vast majority of other projects because my estimated fees were above their budgets. That's even though I only submitted applications or proposals when my qualifications were strong matches with their needs and industries.

Probably the biggest challenge with matchmaking platforms for business services is that they're better suited to less experienced freelancers, gig or side hustle workers. In other words, for career transition workers, part-timers and those really looking for full-time jobs.

Workers living in low-wage countries who can charge cut-rate fees have a big advantage. This is not to say there aren't talented people out there making money via these platforms. However, the current platform-based marketplace is driven more by lowest cost and fast turnaround than by quality and long-term contractor-client relationships. To compensate for very low fees, workers must finish projects very quickly. Quality and customer service are sacrificed at that pace. Also, many of these workers are putting in 60, 70 and even 80 hours a week to earn minimal incomes.

The other major shortfalls of these platforms include: (1) lack of adequate details to develop valid proposals, (2) confusing descriptions of the services needed, (3) unrealistically low budgets, (4) requirements to pay proposal submission fees just to ask questions to prospects, and (5) alerts about projects that have nothing to do with the services listed in the freelancers' profiles. There also are reports where contractors could not get paid or have had their work rejected by clients for no reason with no recourse.

In my experience, I'd say the vast majority of project matchmaking platforms have limited value for professionals who wish to build sustainable businesses. Networking, referrals and strategic marketing are a far more productive. That said, there's no harm in experimenting with an online freelancing platform or two that are compatible with your business and provide credible projects.

I do anticipate that a greater number of better online marketplaces will emerge for solopreneurs and microbusinesses to serve clients who demand quality, value and long-term relationships over lowest cost and fast turnaround only.

43
Marketing to Government Agencies

Bring up the topic of government contracting with a group of solopreneurs or microbusiness people and brace yourself for an outpouring of stories ranging from nightmares to business-saving miracles. The reason for this, from my experience, is because government contracting is unique and challenging in many ways.

I've had mixed success with government contracting. Along the way, I've been awarded very profitable long-term and individual project contracts with federal agencies as well as with a handful of local governments. This work has involved a wide range of my services and even drawn me into new types of services that expanded my client market outside the government realm.

Then again, I've failed to be awarded contracts many times. This was despite the fact that, as I learned later through a bit of research, my proposed team or I was the most qualified applicant. Most times, there was no way to understand the reasoning behind scores for the components of proposals or why another firm was selected with "all things being equal." Other times, their decisions were made strictly on the lowest cost.

First, if you haven't pitched your services to a government entity, you must know that requests for proposals (RFPs) usually are required for government agencies at all levels when the dollar amounts of the contracts exceed certain thresholds. RFPs detail the project, scope of work, vendor requirements and qualifications, schedule and other information about the project. You bid your services and cost based on this information, occasionally with additional details from conference calls, pre-bid meetings and supplemental documentation.

Developing proposals for government entities is time-consuming, so it's expensive for solopreneurs and microbusinesses. Competition for awards usually is tough, due to the number of bidders and the likelihood that you're up against experienced specialists in your category. High-quality proposals give you an opportunity to win, but other factors for awards leave every attempt up to chance.

If your marketing plan includes seeking government contracts, it's best to understand the ecosystem. The following are some important realities about government contracting from my experience and conversations with government contracting and procurement specialists.

- Previous contracts with the agency and for similar projects are a big advantage. Additionally, former agency employees turned contractors often have an inside track for contract awards. Fair or not, these factors can be significant competitive disadvantages for even the most qualified applicants.

- Government agencies usually require certain levels of business insurance, residency requirements, hiring and sub-contracting restrictions, registrations with government vendor-procurement databases, data security specifications, the need to operate as a corporation, and a host of other technical requirements to qualify for awards. These may add overhead costs, limit how you might fulfill contracts, require legal counsel or present any number of issues that could make contracts unaffordable to pursue. Also, there are government payment systems you must be registered with to be approved for contracts.

- To even know about many contracts and respond before deadlines, contractors often need to be signed up for notices from a central federal government system, individual agencies, state procurement systems and local government contract alert lists. Otherwise, you must regularly scan multiple online RFP opportunity platforms for appropriate contracts.

- Proposal scoring looks like an objective process, but subjectivity plays a role, despite the use of averaged scores from evaluators. Opinions, personal and professional bias and other factors affect scoring.

- There are occasions when RFPs are issued only due to the requirement to do so, as preferred contractors already have been identified. There is no way to know when this is the case.

- Some agencies maintain preferred vendor lists, in which applications are submitted to establish pre-qualified status for approved vendors. This may be announced by RFPs or you must inquire.

My four most important tips for increasing your success with government contracting are: (1) only focus on **RFPs** that align very well with your qualifications and project experience, (2) answer all questions and respond to every requirement in your proposals even if they don't seem to apply to your business to prevent disqualification by being deemed "unresponsive," (3) be persuasive about how well you understand the project and the function of the agency, and (4) include solutions and content that set you apart from your competition.

Of course, you cannot market your services to government agencies if you don't know about the opportunities. The U.S. federal contract listing service is FedBizOpps.gov. Some individual federal agencies also have their own contract opportunity Web sites. Each state has its own contract listing Web site, with many including county and city opportunities as well. Typically, you can sign up for alerts for your field or types of services to keep up on requests for proposals (RFPs) and requests for qualifications (RFQs).

Another avenue for government contracting is to market your services to companies that have GSA Schedule contracts. These are companies that have gone through a somewhat complex process to establish what is basically prequalified status through the General Services Administration's Multiple Award Program. It's a sort of insider system apart from normal RFPs and RFQs postings. You would offer your services to these companies as a sub-contractor. This can be far simpler and productive than applying for your own GSA Schedule unless your focus is on government clients.

If you've worked for or with government agencies in the past, you might have an advantage over the competition. Even if you haven't had experience with this market, you should take the time to investigate agencies and contract award lists to determine if there are good opportunities for you to pursue. Government work can be lucrative and provide ongoing contracts if you find the right niche for your services.

44
Co-Working Space Use for Client Prospecting

A co-working space can provide interesting possibilities for your marketing efforts, albeit a somewhat unconventional approach. In these facilities, there are far more opportunities for interaction with resident entrepreneurs than in traditional office buildings. The right mix of resident entrepreneurs could offer the chance to work with startups and other microbusinesses. Co-working facilities tend to be used most by software developers, technology product creators, product designers and remote workers with various specialties.

First, would it be a prudent business decision for you to incur the expense of renting or leasing space in a co-working facility. Does such an office make sense for your type of business, either part-time or full-time? Is your workstyle a good fit with a co-working ecosystem? Is there a local facility that houses legitimate prospects for your services? Since a high percentage of prospects will be startups, are you willing to customize payment, equity, mentorship or other arrangements to fit their budgets? Does the facility promote mixers or other mechanisms for residents to meet and collaborate?

The most obvious outsourced service needs for startups and microbusinesses might include the following: accounting, marketing, procurement, sales, venture funding consulting, graphic design, Web development, legal guidance, business consulting, staffing and public relations.

Importantly, your primary intent to operate at a co-working facility cannot be just to market your services to other residents. Your outreach efforts may or may not be effective. Also, it might take some time to build relationships with residents and convert them to clients.

One way to enhance your visibility would be to offer free or low-cost workshops on hot topics for the types of businesses based in the facility. Free one-hour consultations might draw significant interest, as well. Being friendly to and curious about residents will go a long way to establish relationships. However, I suspect that an aggressive sales approach won't be successful due to the nature of co-working facility cultures.

Another option for location-based marketing is to frequent public spaces such as coffee shops, cafés, libraries or public college campuses. Without being overly aggressive or intrusive, you can listen to nearby conversations or notice the types of work others are doing. This way, you can look for opportunities to start conversations.

Ideally, you can get your work done in these places because you never know how productive this marketing approach will be on any given day.

45
Opportunities With Project Wrap-Ups and Post-Mortems

The end of a project can be the beginning of a long-term business relationship if you wrap it up properly. Unfortunately, too many professionals send final thank you messages by email or online payment systems when they submit their last invoice. That's it. No marketing effort is made.

This is an opportunity to conduct a project post-mortem and wrap-up, with the detail level in line with the size of the project. A short or small project deserves a couple of paragraphs to cite what went well, any valuable lessons learned and what could be improved the next time you work together. A bigger or longer-term project contains this same content in more depth, along with relevant data on the process and maybe recommendations for follow-up by the client.

In all cases, some language in the write-ups should reflect your work in a way that connects you more deeply to the client than just in terms of this one-off project. For example, there may be a place to include phrases such as, "The next time we collaborate on a project like this…" You're trying to convey the message that you want to work more with the client.

Another important action to take at the end of a project is to do what seems obvious but rarely is done by contractors: ask if a similar project is planned. There is no better time to position yourself for a follow-on project or new one than at the tail end of a successful engagement.

It's tough for most of us to ask a question like this, as it's so sales oriented. One way to make it easier to ask is to personalize it. For example, "I really enjoyed working with you on this project and we achieved great results. If there are other projects in the works with which I could assist you, I'd appreciate the opportunity to develop a proposal for you." Remember that contractor-client relationships are just that, relationships. An open communication channel, previously earned trust and past mutual success with work provide an effective opportunity to secure future contracts.

A twist on the previous strategy of asking about more work is to request an internal referral. This involves asking your client if he/she is aware of appropriate projects that are being launched by colleagues and if you could be introduced to those project leads. Internal referrals like these are powerful. You enter project discussions with a direct or implied endorsement, as well as already being in the procurement and accounting system and having proven knowledge of the company's business.

Your final couple of communications with clients also should ensure that they know about your other services. They probably only know you for the expertise you provided so they might not think beyond that. With your inside knowledge, you should be aware of two or three potential applications of your other services for their business. Always make sure clients are aware of your full range of services, ideally right from the start of projects.

I consider the end of one project as the start of ongoing marketing communication with clients, as long as we have a good relationship. I use emails or occasional calls that open with a brief reference to the past projects just to help them remember me. My comfort zone is to frame this type of communication as staying in touch, sharing information that might be of interest to former clients or alerting them to potential opportunities. The closing soft-sell component is just something like, "I look forward to working with you again soon. Please let me know if you'd like to chat about a project or have me submit a proposal."

We all know how much easier it is to sell past or existing clients on using our services again than it is to acquire new clients. That fact should make this bit of sales more palatable.

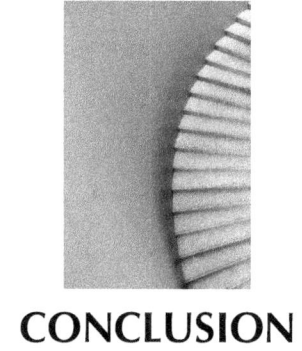

CONCLUSION

46
Your Marketing Success Formula

As a solopreneur or microbusiness, you have two big competitive advantages over larger service providers. One is how you can respond and adapt your services very quickly to changes in your marketplace. The other is how you can customize and personalize your marketing to client niches. And both of these advantages can be at the core of your value marketing plan.

A global marketplace, technology and trends toward increased use of contracted services have accelerated change in nearly every industry. Pain points—markets for your solutions—appear, evolve and disappear rapidly. This dynamic ecosystem provides great opportunities for professionals who anticipate and respond quickly to the needs of prospective and existing clients.

You can adapt your business' services to clients' new pain points as well as create new services to be in the right place at the right time for the niches you serve. With little cost and risk, you can experiment with different packaging of services. You can test new types of services in your marketplace to see which ones offer the best potential.

Some services might fail and others succeed, but you'll always gain valuable lessons to stay competitive in the marketplace. In other words, your business can operate at the forefront of service providers in your field by adopting a strategy of being adaptable, resilient and resourceful.

The other advantage you have is how you can focus on customizing and personalizing your marketing. These efforts can be grounded in the value you have to offer and relationships you can build that lead to contracts. You don't need dozens of contracts to pay for expensive overhead costs. Quality, not quantity, can be your strategy. By quality I mean larger, longer, expanding and more profitable contracts with your preferred clients.

Your customized and personalized marketing efforts can accomplish this. Strategic investment of time in research and conversations will result in superior pitches and proposals, as well as opportunities through referrals. You have the luxury of selecting niche markets, understanding how to engage them, build a platform to become visible to them and establish sustainable connections one-by-one.

In this way, smart marketing will serve as an effective way to communicate how your skills, knowledge and experience can solve your clients' problems and foster mutually successful outcomes.

I wish you the pleasure of meaningful work and prosperity on your solo or micro entrepreneurial journey.

47
About the Author

Douglas Freeman has been a self-employed entrepreneur for over three decades. He co-founded his company Ideascape, Inc. with his wife and fellow entrepreneur, MacKenzie. Recently, they launched Imaginexxus LLC as a publishing business for their unconventional travel books and products. Douglas also co-founded four other startups with partners. These included a book publishing company, business documentary production firm, innovation think tank and entertainment development company.

Over the years, Douglas has adapted his services to market trends and personal interests. His work has included all types of technical and non-technical business, marketing, educational, training, public relations, ghostwriting, media development work as well as creative and consulting services. He has served clients ranging from NASA, the U.S. Department of Energy, U.S. Department of the Interior and the Armed Forces Network to Intel, Hewlett-Packard, T-Mobile and Southern Company. Additionally, he has worked with scores of startups, small businesses, local government agencies and non-profit organizations.

Douglas has earned regional and national awards for his technical writing, video scriptwriting and media productions. These include Telly Awards, a NASA Achievement Award and a U.S. Department of Energy Exceptional Public Service Award. His educational videos on entrepreneurship were selected for presentation at film festivals in three countries. Douglas' previous book *Workarounds: 50+ insider tactics for age 50+ entrepreneurs* has been reviewed and had excerpts published by

Forbes, PBS Next Avenue, Freelancers Union, Good Reads and other platforms.

Douglas invites you to share your marketing and entrepreneurship experiences with him. He may include your story in one of his posts or articles published on LinkedIn, Twitter and Medium. Contact him via his Web site at www.ideascapeinc.com, LinkedIn at www.linkedin.com/in/dougatideascapeinc and Twitter at @ideascapeinc.

To keep up on Douglas' latest posts and articles, you can follow him on any of those social network platforms.

www.ingramcontent.com/pod-product-compliance
Lightning Source LLC
Chambersburg PA
CBHW071543220526
45469CB00003B/899